THE INTERNET SEARCHER'S HANDBOOK

LOCATING
INFORMATION
PEOPLE
& SOFTWARE

YO-CDR-854

Peter Morville, Louis Rosenfeld, and Joseph Janes

NEAL-SCHUMAN NETGUIDE SERIES

Neal-Schuman Publishers, Inc.

New York   London

Published by Neal-Schuman Publishers, Inc.
100 Varick Street
New York, NY 10013

Printed and bound in the United States of America.

Library of Congress Cataloging-in-Publication Data

Morville, Peter.
   The Internet searcher's handbook : locating information, people, and software / by Peter Morville, Louis Rosenfeld, Joseph Janes.
     p. cm.
   Includes bibliographical references and index.
   ISBN 1-55570-236-8 (alk. paper)
    1. Internet (Computer Network) 2. Computer network resources.
I. Rosenfeld, Louis B. II. Janes, Joseph. III. Title.
TK5105.875.I57M668   1996
025.04—dc20   95-47670

Contents

Foreword

by Richard Wiggins

Brewster Kahle—the inventor of an important Internet indexing and search mechanism called WAIS—tells a story about an Internet demonstration he gave at San Francisco's science museum, the Exploratorium. A variety of young people tried their hands at surfing the Internet and at finding the specific things they might want to learn more about. Then, one boy said "I'd like to ask the Internet a question."

Kahle explained to the young man that sadly, the Internet isn't that sort of critter. First off, there isn't any one place on the Internet to which you should present your question; you have to pick a particular information resource, then submit your query to that service—using the search language that facility expects. But wouldn't it be nice, Kahle wonders, if indeed users could simply ask the Internet a question—and expect a reasonable answer?

That sort of simple model has been the dream of computer users as long as we've had on-line systems. Shouldn't we be able to ask the Internet all sorts of questions?

- "How many acres of corn were planted in Iowa last year?"
- "What is the population of Senegal?"
- "What is the e-mail address for the admissions office at Auburn University?"
- "How did Congressman Ehlers vote on the telecommunications bill last month?"
- "What books did C.S. Lewis write?"
- "Show me a picture of Comet Shoemaker-Levy hitting Jupiter."
- "What television programs are dedicated to Internet topics?"

These are all questions for which one can find answers on the Internet. Unfortunately, though, we can't just present these questions to a single, all-encompassing Internet interface and get the answers we're looking for. As a global network of networks, the Internet has far too many information resources, and too diverse a set of information publishing tools, for things to be that simple.

Fictional computer systems would have no problem handling our example questions. A "Star Trek" character would simply say "computer" and ask any of these questions, and the machine would reply with the answer desired—delivered promptly and with smooth, modulated inflection. No computer today is that friendly and helpful, but a number of visionaries believe the day will soon arrive when on-line systems will achieve that level of responsiveness to our needs.

In fact, vendors of information technology software have tried for years to implement such systems. Ten years ago the goal was to devise "natural language" query mechanisms that sat atop existing databases. Today, the mantra is the "information agent"—a tool that roams the Net, monitoring, gathering, filtering, and presenting information on our behalf. Tom Selleck's voice-over on those "You Will" commercials tells us that AT&T will provide the right tools. Numerous startup companies say they'll win the race. Some of us believe that information agents have been oversold, and that we're a long way off from carrying out productive voice conversations with our on-line systems.

In the meantime, we have to live in today's world. There are some analogies between how you find what you want on the Internet and how you find things in a traditional library. You wouldn't walk into a bricks-and-mortar library and, standing in the vestibule, begin shouting your question, expecting that answers would flow forth from the building itself. From our early schooldays onward, we're taught how to exploit the standard reference resources of the library—when to go to the *Readers' Guide to Periodical Literature*, when to explore the *Encyclopaedia Britannica*, when to consult an unabridged dictionary, when to search the catalog (these days probably an on-line catalog, not a card catalog), and when to ask a reference librarian.

Similarly, when you want to find something on the Internet, you have to have some understanding of the standard reference materials and the catalogs that are at your disposal. You also have to phrase the question appropriately for the catalog you're trying to consult. If the Internet is a virtual library, this book is your guided tour of the reference department and the catalog.

In 1898 Halsey William Wilson found that his job as a bookseller was too complicated: keeping up with all the titles he might want for his inventory meant reading through numerous publishers' catalogs. He decided to create a *single* catalog, which he christened the *Cumulative Book Index*. Today H.W. Wilson and Company remains an important vendor of library indexes. (You can read more about this story on the World Wide Web—visit *http://www.hwwilson.com/history.html*).

In 1993, one of the authors of this book, Lou Rosenfeld, saw a need for a *single* place where people could go to find resources on the Internet. He formed the *Clearinghouse for Subject-Oriented Internet Resource Guides* at the University of Michigan. His goal was to have librarians and other Internet scouts collaborate to build a high-quality compendium of bibliographies. Today, the Clearinghouse is co-sponsored by Argus Associates and the University of Michigan. The managing editor of the Clearinghouse is the primary author of this text, Peter Morville. Rosenfeld and Morville are now the principals of Argus Associates, which seeks to do for the Internet community the sorts of things H.W. Wilson sought to do for the print publishing world at the turn of the last century.

The people at Argus Associates are not alone in this *fin de siècle* quest, of course. The names of Internet index tools are becoming part of the popular lexicon—first Archie, then Veronica, then Yahoo, and Webcrawler and Lycos. Corresponding to many of these names are highly successful commercial enterprises. The early successes of these ventures testify as to the importance of tools that help Internet users find what they're looking for.

Of course, not all of your Internet expeditions will involve "serious" searches for answers. Sometimes people like to browse casually through information sources, which is why even major research libraries usually offer a browsing collection. Some people enjoy spending time skimming through dictionaries or encyclopedias—but those reading sessions are enjoyable only if you understand the landscape of the document you're reading. This book will help you understand the landscape of the Internet, so that you will find peripatetic browsing of the Net enjoyable and even serendipitous.

Peter Deutsch, the co-inventor of Archie, says that he and his colleagues, collaborators and competitors are trying to re-invent 100 years of library science—this time in an Internet context. *The Internet Searcher's Handbook* will be uniquely useful because its authors are not just toolsmiths, but also scholars in the field of library science. Their discussion brings the singular insights of people who have helped advance the state of Internet catalogs—from the perspective of library and information sciences.

We eagerly await a new millennium and a new era in on-line information retrieval—the day when that boy can "ask the Internet a question" and get the answers he needs. In the meantime, let *The Internet Searcher's Handbook* be your guide to the reality of resource discovery on today's Internet. Whether your goal is casual browsing or purposeful searching, your voyages will yield more fruit as a result of this book.

Note: An HTML version of this foreword (with appropriate hypertext links) is available via the World Wide Web at *http://www.msu.edu/staff/rww/srchfore.html*.

Richard Wiggins, 1995
Author of *The Internet for Everyone: A Guide for Users and Providers*

Preface

"Errors like straws, upon the surface flow;
He who would search for pearls must dive below"
— Dryden

At surface level, the Internet appears as a shimmering ocean of digital information. Professional journals, literary classics, national news services, stock reports, virtual communities, image databases, and digital libraries are just some of the wonders awaiting the uninitiated. Graphical browsers provide intuitive point–and–click access. Powerful search tools combine with intelligent software agents to put a global network of information at your fingertips.

Yet, dive beneath the surface and you'll soon find yourself lost in the Internet's murky depths. Complex mazes of hypertext links, user-hostile search tools, and countless numbers of low-quality resources can quickly discourage beginners who find themselves "drowning in information."

Fortunately, in the past few years a diverse group of tools for resource discovery on the Internet has become available. Unfortunately, it's often difficult to find and use these tools. Each tool serves a slightly different purpose, documentation is often poor or non-existent, and the collection of tools is constantly evolving. This book is intended to provide the searcher with an understanding of the principles of on-line searching and detailed knowledge of the current tools for Internet information retrieval. It is our hope that this combination of the conceptual with the practical will forge an understanding that outlives the tools of today and carries the searcher into the brave new information society of tomorrow.

The first half of this book will explain how to use the Internet for finding information, people, and software. In **Fundamentals of Searching Digital Resources**, Joseph Janes discusses the basic principles of on-line searching and explains how they apply in the Internet environment. If you've ever wondered how Boolean logic works or what it means to perform proximity and adjacency searching, this chapter is for you. In **Using the Internet for Reference**, Sara Ryan covers the ins and outs of executing ad hoc queries. *What's the capital of Bolivia? What's the current price of Netscape stock? What's the URL for Tufts University?* Sara explains how to answer all these questions and more. In **Using the Internet for Research**, Peter Morville shows how to conduct more extensive on-line investigations. For those looking for as much information as possible on the topic of biotechnology or rainforest ecology or personal finance, this chapter will explain how to get started. Finally, in **Online Communities as Tools for Research and Reference**, Louis Rosenfeld discusses the valuable role communities of people can play in facilitating Internet searching. He explains how to find the right groups of people and how to interact successfully with these groups by respecting the unwritten rules of "netiquette."

The second half of this book is devoted to detailed descriptions and evaluations of the most useful tools and resources for Internet searching. Meta-information such as title, use, searching tips, strengths, and weaknesses is provided for each resource. Sample searches are included to further illuminate the most effective use of each tool. The tools are organized into three primary categories: virtual libraries, Internet directories, and Internet search tools. While there is significant overlap in the characteristics and uses of these tools, the distinctions between them are important to keep in mind. *Virtual libraries* or "value added collections of Internet resources" are the closest net-based equivalent to traditional libraries. Through the identification, selection, organization, description, and evaluation of resources, "digital librarians" or "cybrarians" have created collections of pointers to valuable information resources. Users may browse through these libraries, looking for information on a particular topic. *Internet directories* or "collections of resources maintained by the global Internet community" are the most comprehensive and popular of today's Internet tool set. Most directories allow anyone to add or publish information. Directories provide an organizational hierarchy to facilitate browsing and often compliment the subject tree with a search interface. Finally, *Internet search tools* constitute the richest and most diverse category. Users interact with search tools via query interfaces that range from the simple to the sophisticated. The search tools are divided into those that are useful for finding information, software, people, and communities of people.

It is inevitable that the tools and resources section of this book will become dated. Today's tools will evolve, move to new locations, or even cease to exist. New tools will be developed to take their places. Internet directories will appropriate the strengths and capabilities of virtual libraries and search tools, and vice versa. This book is static, but the Internet is highly dynamic. For this reason, we have developed the *Internet Searching Center* (http://www.lib.umich.edu/chouse/searching/find.html), an on-line collection of pointers to all of the tools and resources covered in this book. As the old tools move or disappear and new tools arise, we will make changes accordingly. The *Internet Searching Center* will serve as an Internet-based companion to this book.

Chapter One

Fundamentals of Searching Digital Resources

by Joseph Janes, Ph.D.
Director, Internet Public Library and Assistant Professor
School of Information and Library Studies,
University of Michigan

INTRODUCTION

Here's a common experience: after hearing all the hype from newspapers, magazines, television, friends, and so on, someone finally decides to get connected and find out what this Internet thing is all about. After the initial disorientation, the first few hours are spent in excitement and discovery. Wow—here's somebody's home page in Australia. Gee—I found a Web site in Hungary that gives opera schedules all over the world. Look—here's the full text of the Japanese constitution on this Gopher. Hey—I can send e-mail to the President of the United States.

That excitement often fades after the first few forays into the Net. Web sites are down or have huge images that take forever to load. Gophers aren't maintained. The President doesn't answer your brilliant message about global warming. One of the most common complaints, though, is that it's so darn hard to *find* anything out there. Sure, it's fun to surf and explore, but if you actually wanted something on a specific topic, say, evolution, it can be difficult if not impossible to find it. This kind of postprandial frustration leads many people to believe that the Net is a swirling mass, interesting for some people, but certainly not a place for serious research or a stable environment for finding information.

To an extent, of course, this is true. But it is also true that there are many very valuable sources of information in this new networked environment which are difficult to find anywhere else. The frustration comes from the ease of using standard information tools, like reference books, library catalogs, indexes, and so on, which are familiar and provide high-quality information. The Net just isn't like that, and probably won't be for quite a while. The Net has its own unique characteristics, and understanding them will help considerably in using the tools and resources available to find specific information.

In this chapter, we will discuss the various types of systems and tools available both commercially and on the Net and the differences between them, briefly review the fundamentals of searching and preparation using digital products, and conclude with a discussion of search features, the current state of searching on the Net and some thoughts about the future.

WHY ARE YOU SEARCHING?

The first question you need to ask yourself, regardless of the setting or type of information resources you want to explore, is whether "searching" is the right approach to take. There are many instances where "searching," in the sense of entering commands to an information retrieval system to identify items which may be of interest or value, is not the best method.

If you are looking for *particular* items—a specific book or article, a certain person's home page or phone number or e-mail address, or financial information about a group of companies—then direct searching may be the only way to proceed. If, on the other hand, you are looking more broadly, for example for a few books or articles or Internet resources on a topic, then you may wish to browse the stacks of a library, surf the Internet for a while, or use other tools designed to give an overview rather than "the" definitive answer or answers.

Often a mix of strategies is best, but it is always wise to remember that "searching" per se may not be your only answer. Librarians have long been familiar with the distinction between using systems like Dialog or Lexis, and browsing in a catalog or CD-ROM, but the distributed networked environment of the Internet is still another world to many people. In fact, there are some resources currently available and widely used on the Net which incorporate both browsing and searching. Furthermore, many of the features and commands familiar in library catalog systems, CD-ROM products, and other commercial digital information resources are only beginning to emerge in the networked world.

NETWORKED INFORMATION RESOURCES

The range of information resources available in digital formats, either exclusively, primarily, or as companion versions of print resources, grows daily. We are now accustomed to library catalogs in digital form, often incorporating access to other tools as well (journal indexes, for example). Similarly, access to databases via commercial vendors and CD-ROMs is commonplace.

New genres of resources are arising though, in the distributed networked environment, many of which have no print analogs or which share little with the more stable and familiar sources described above. It is important to understand something about the nature of these new sources and how they differ from their ancestors to be able to use them, search them, and decide when they might be most appropriate.

The Environment

The two most important things to understand about the networked world are these: it is a *distributed* environment, and it is a *dynamic* environment. These two different but related characteristics define this world and help you to know how to best use it and live in it.

By "distributed," we mean that it has no center, no overall authority, no tangible sense of coherence. There are thousands upon thousands of computers connected to the Internet, each of which has the capability to make information resources available, instantly and in most cases free of charge, to a global audience in the millions. Nobody can stop you, once you're connected, from putting up a home page, Web site, Gopher, FTP site, whatever you like. This unprecedented freedom to publish and communicate ideas clearly has enormous potential for intellectual exchange and the sharing of knowledge.

Furthermore, this environment is dynamic. Each of these resources can change by the second. New ones arise daily; other ones move or become unavailable for one reason or another. Most are not updated that rapidly (and indeed, many are never updated, raising altogether different problems), but the potential for nearly instantaneous responsiveness and creativity is also exciting.

It's also a pain in the neck. Since there are virtually no controls over who can put what out there, things change continually, and since there are no standards for what librarians think of as intellectual control (cataloging, indexing, organization, etc.), it's a mess. It can be fun and challenging and occasionally enlightening to simply wander around, surfing through the contours of the Net, coming across all sorts of new and different things. But there's also a lot of worthless, idiosyncratic garbage, and finding good stuff (or indeed anything at all) on a particular topic can be difficult, at best. This is why the Net is often referred to as a chaotic world, and it's an apt description. Most of the things that we take for granted in the world of books, libraries, and commercial information products exist in crude, simplistic forms or not at all.

Net Resources v. Standard Commercial Resources

Many of the differences we can identify between Net versus standard commercial sources stem from the lack of standards in the networked world. The freedom and flexibility offered by the Net have not yet given way or forced the development of standard information structures, search facilities, styles, and so on. There is a growing appreciation among many people who create and use Net resources that such things are important, and a few tentative steps have been taken, but little has yet become established.

Several characteristics of networked resources are worth noting in more detail:

- **Dynamism:** Although we mentioned this above, it's worth restating. We are not used to books or articles or other print resources which change overnight. To be sure, databases are continually updated and new editions are common, but the nature of these changes are less dramatic than what is found on the Net. It is not unusual, on a typical day of working with networked resources, to find that one has changed its address (and, with luck, has left a link leading you to the new location), another has been updated and thus the interface has changed, a third is gone entirely because its creator has graduated from college and no longer maintains it, and a new one has come up with a great deal of interesting material. This is something of an exaggeration; not every resource changes every day, but the degree and speed of change on the network are often disorienting.
- **Quality, Review, Authority:** An article does not get published in the *New England Journal of Medicine* or any other scholarly journal without undergoing a rigorous process of peer review and approval. Books do not get published by Random House or major houses without editing both their content and style. Entries are not added to databases like Sociological Abstracts without being checked that they conform with indexing and other policies.
  These sorts of checks on style, grammar, authority, and quality have not been widely implemented in the networked world. There

are some scholarly journals which appear in electronic form and a few attempts have been made to enforce standards on other resources, but in general it is *caveat lector*—let the reader beware. Many people are aware of the need of such procedures to make the Net an attractive and worthwhile medium for serious communication and sharing of knowledge, but the lack of central authority and consensus have so far prevented anything from taking hold.

- **Currency:** Despite the fact that networked resources can be updated with ease, many aren't. It is easy to create a resource and even easier to leave it alone once it is up. Maintaining, updating, and developing networked resources is a continual challenge, and one which not all creators meet successfully. Again, a great many resources are up-to-date and current, and thus very useful; and for others, continual updating is not necessary, but it can be a problem in some cases.

This, then, is the environment in which any searcher must operate in trying to identify potentially valuable information on the Net. It is not as completely hopeless as it may sound from this discussion. A number of tools have been developed which can make finding things easier. (Individual and more extensive discussions of these can be found later in this book.)

NET SEARCH TOOLS

Broadly stated, there are three major categories of search tools on the Net: virtual libraries or catalogs, Internet directories, and search tools. The first two are primarily browsing tools, although many incorporate search features; the third is primarily for specific searching. The terminology of "catalogs" such as the Whole Internet Catalog, "directories" like Yahoo, and "libraries" such as the World Wide Web (or WWW, or W_3) Virtual Library is still fluid, and it would not be unusual to find the same resource called by any of these three names. They tend to differ on the degree of consistency and coherence they provide, as well as, functionality, editorial control, and focus.

Preparing to Search

As with any searches in the print or commercial digital domain, a search on the Net requires several steps of preparation: understanding the topic or topics of interest, extracting one or more concepts inherent in the question, identifying potentially useful terms which adequately represent those concepts, selecting possible resources and tools to use, and executing the search.

Again, it is important to acknowledge the environment in which the search will take place in many of these steps. For example, since there are few standards of indexing, classification, or vocabulary control in networked resources, it is almost always impossible to use any controlled vocabularies or thesauri. Familiar tools such as the Library of Congress Subject Headings or the Thesaurus of Psychological Index Terms are of little help. Rather, colloquial expressions, slang, metaphorical uses of words, and nonstandard writing are often seen on the Net, and may either obscure potentially useful resources or combine with content words and thus produce larger retrieval sets. Furthermore, since much of what exists on the Net revolves around the Net itself and computing more generally, searching on words like "Internet," "Net," "computer," "archive," "software," and so on is typically useless.

This all means that decision-making on the part of the searcher becomes even more critical. In fact, many of these decisions are similar to those familiar to most librarians. What are the best resources to use in this circumstance, based on experience with the tools, coverage of various resources, features available for use, constraints of time and money, quality of the information, reputation of the source, and so on? The questions don't really change all that much. This sort of professional assessment of the environment and how best to work within it, though, becomes even more important in such a chaotic and dynamic climate.

SEARCH FEATURES

There are a number of features available in most commercial or library systems which experienced (and not-so-experienced) searchers can use to refine or improve the quality of their searching. These features have evolved over the years as technologies have grown more sophisticated, and they require a substantial amount of preparation and work to implement. In this section, we'll discuss the more important of these, and see whether they can be used in the networked environment.

First, though, we must explore how information is stored inside the system to facilitate searching and retrieval. We'll use the commercial information system, Dialog, as an example. When a command is given within Dialog to find documents containing a given word, say WILL, the system will not search the full text of each document in the database looking for this word. Rather, it will consult the inverted file (in Dialog this is called the Basic Index), which is a list of all words found in documents in the database, along with pointers to where those words occur. So, it can report that the word WILL is found in X documents in the Y database relatively quickly, much more quickly than having to search through all the full texts. Dialog allows searchers to conduct much more extensive and sophisticated searches, because its designers constructed inverted files to support these advanced techniques. Some of these features are available in some Internet-based tools; many aren't yet.

Truncation

It may be that the searcher really is looking for information on wills (in the sense of last will and testament), and so may wish to find documents containing the word WILL but also the word WILLS. Many systems support truncation, which allows the searcher to specify that documents must contain at least a particular character string. In Dialog, this is represented by the question mark, so a search on WILL? will produce all documents containing words that begin with WILL, such as WILL, WILLS, WILLY, WILLPOWER, and so on. This broader search will probably gather most of the documents in the database on wills (and potentially a number of other topics as well). Truncation is a powerful tool, but also has some obvious side effects. Indeed, Dialog has several truncation commands, and an experienced searcher would probably choose to search on WILL? ?, indicating a wish for only one additional character, rather than an arbitrary number.

Truncation is actually rather common in network-based tools, but is not always obvious, may be called other things, and might even be invisible. For example, the Lycos search engine automatically truncates. Typing WILL in Lycos will get you all the variants listed above automatically. You actually have to actively ask it *not* to truncate by adding a period to the ends of words: WILL. will look only for the word "will" in documents.

It's common to see search engines ask if you wish to search for your words as complete words or substrings. *Substring* is a term from computer science, and it means that the series of characters you ask for will occur somewhere in the word but not necessarily at the beginning. (Experienced searchers will recognize that this amounts to implicit left-hand *and* right-hand truncation.) So a substring search in Yahoo, for example, on WILL will produce all the other variations as well as TWILL, SWILL, TERWILLIGER, etc. This will produce even more false retrievals. Asking to search as complete words stops truncation altogether; there is often no middle ground.

Boolean searching

Suppose the topic of interest is actually living wills. In this case, the searcher wants documents which have not only the word WILL in some form but also the word LIVING. In Dialog, this can easily be accomplished by using the Boolean operator AND: LIVING AND WILL? produces the set of documents containing the word LIVING and any word beginning with WILL. The other two Boolean operators, OR (used to combine spelling variations, synonyms, and related words) and NOT (used to eliminate terms) are also available.

Boolean searching is often seen in networked tools, but usually in less-developed forms. Veronica, the search tool used in Gophers, allows actually for quite sophisticated searching: LIVING AND WILL° works in Veronica, where the asterisk is the truncation operator.

Some systems, such as Yahoo and WebCrawler, use implicit Boolean operators. Typing LIVING WILL in either one is equivalent to using an AND between them, although in both cases, it can be turned off. Then it becomes an implicit OR. In some cases, though, Boolean searching is not available, as is discussed below.

Adjacency

Experienced online searchers will know that Dialog can do better than LIVING AND WILL? for this search. Using the proximity operator, we can specify that these two words must appear next to each other, in this order, for a document to be retrieved. Asking for LIVING(W)WILL? would not retrieve documents which mention, for example, Will Rogers in one sentence, and his living room in another, since AND alone only requires that the two words be in the same document, whether they have anything to do with each other or not.

Many Internet search tools appear as though they provide this feature. WAIS, Lycos, InfoSeek—all of these allow searchers to type words and phrases, and magically produce retrievals. However, these systems allow neither Boolean operators (words such as AND and OR are either ignored or searched themselves!) nor adjacency searching. They employ algorithms which look for the target words in documents and then calculate scores for each based on several factors—for example, how often the words occur, whether they occur early or late in documents or in titles, whether they occur close together, their overall frequency, and so on. Some of these formulas are quite complex, and they are often hidden from the user. So typing LIVING WILL at Lycos, for example, produces a ranked list of documents ranging from *living, learning, and working in California* to *living art center in Sweden*, all of which include WILL in one sense or another. These systems are quite powerful and often produce good results, but it can be a bit disconcerting, especially to those experienced with commercial systems, not to be able to have more control over the retrievals they produce.

Fields & Context

In Dialog, there are a great many other commands at the searcher's disposal. We'll discuss only two more: the ability to search for words in particular fields of the document (the title, the abstract, the index terms) and the ability to focus a search based on the context of documents (say, only retrieving documents from particular years or in particular languages). One might see a search such as this:

(LIVING(W)WILL? ?)/TI AND PY=1995

which would look for the phrase "living will" or "living wills" in the title field in documents published in 1995.

These features are pretty much unknown on the Internet as yet. It is likely that something like this will arise as more time and effort are spent on developing search facilities, but at the moment, only a few rudimentary features of this sort are available. Lycos allows searchers to indicate a minimum score, below which documents will not be presented. Yahoo's search engine permits searches to be restricted somewhat by field.

The reason these are only appearing slowly if at all is the amount of work required to make them available. Not only do the search engines need to be designed, but inverted files must be sophisticated enough to support searching of words together, in specific fields. Documents must include tags about dates, languages, authorship, and other contextual information. Then there is the whole question of indexing, classification, and name authority, so common in familiar library systems, which is only now dawning on the Net world. There is clearly a long way to go to make these systems as reliable and powerful as those found in the commercial realm.

THE FUTURE

It's clear that for the enormous potential of the Internet to allow people and communities to share information to be more fully realized, better search tools must be developed. Current tools, such as Lycos, Webcrawler, Veronica, and Yahoo are not nearly as comprehensive as those often seen in commercial information retrieval systems. However, they are steadily improving. For example, the Open Text search engine on the Web allows for Boolean searching as well as providing a number of other more developed features.

As system designers continue to explore the possibilities of the networked environment, and users begin to demand more precise search capabilities, this trend will continue. And this environment will improve even more quickly as people with library and other information backgrounds become more notable participants in not just the use but the development of these tools. Their experiences in using search tools, as well as working with users to understand their topics and identify potentially useful terms, understanding information resources and their organization, and making appropriate connections between the two, will be invaluable in the design of the next generations of searching tools.

Chapter Two

Using the Internet for Reference

by Sara Ryan, M.I.L.S.
Reference Center Coordinator
Internet Public Library

INTRODUCTION

Reference librarians in traditional libraries use a multitude of sources to answer the questions they are asked. However, some resources stand out as being both the most useful and the most frequently consulted. This collection of resources is known as the "ready reference collection," and is kept close to the reference desk. Resources in the ready reference collection help librarians and library users answer a relatively large percentage of factual questions such as the following:

- What is the address of the Institute of Electrical and Electronics Engineers?
- What is the chemical composition of Agent Orange?
- What's the average annual rainfall in the Amazon rain forest?

People can answer these questions quickly and efficiently using the ready reference collection, without having to venture into the stacks to search.

You might think you could answer factual questions of this type even more quickly by using the Internet. You would not be entirely wrong, but neither would you be entirely correct. Anyone who thinks that the Internet can provide the answer to every reference question hasn't been using the Internet for very long. Even if the answer is available on the Internet, it may take hours or days to find.

But why is this? We hear constantly that we're living in the information age, and that the Internet is one of the largest repositories of information currently in existence. Why shouldn't we be able to find information quickly on the Internet?

It will be easier to understand this seeming paradox if we contrast the search *process* in traditional libraries with the process that is necessary when we search for information on the Internet.

Someone using a world almanac to answer a question such as "What is the average annual rainfall in the Amazon rain forest?" merely has to walk to the shelf, take the book down, check the index to find the page where the desired information is printed, and find the answer.

Imagine how much longer the search would take if that same person had to go through a process like this:

- Ascertain whether something calling itself a "World Almanac" exists, (and if it doesn't, try to think of other things a resource containing the needed information might be called).
- Find out where it is in the library (without using a card catalog).
- Once the book is in hand, find out whether it contains the answer to the question. (The book may or may not have an index...)

That process is analogous to the way we have to search for information on the Internet.

This is not to say that it's always faster and easier to use print sources—otherwise we wouldn't be writing this, would we? There is a growing set of questions that relate directly to the Internet and thus can be best answered using Internet resources:

- What is the address of Microsoft's homepage?
- How do I send e-mail to the White House?
- Where can I find the latest version of the Netscape software?

There are also questions that people have been asking for years that can be answered more quickly and/or more cheaply using Internet resources:

- What's the current price of IBM stock?
- What does the acronym ASME stand for?
- What is the Japanese language translation for "feather"?

Certainly you can answer all of these questions using traditional print resources, but if you know where to look, it's much faster to answer them using the Internet.

We'll talk about where to look, and how to evaluate what you've found, a little later in this chapter. Right now we'll provide a few sample scenarios to compare and contrast Internet reference tools with the traditional print resources found in a typical library.

Example One

Glen wants to find the name of Connecticut's state flower.

The best reference tool for answering this question would be a current almanac. Most libraries have at least one almanac in their ready reference collection. A reader can pick up the book, scan the index, and provide the answer, much as outlined above, in a few minutes. This question could probably be answered using the Internet, but the search might take from several minutes to several hours. Until the Internet is blessed with the free, searchable, full text of a current almanac, questions like this will be far more easily answered using traditional reference tools.

Example Two

Sharon wants to know if the Bantam Doubleday Dell publishing company has a public site on the World Wide Web.

An excellent reference tool for answering this question is Open Market's Directory of Commercial Services. Sharon can go to Open Market's homepage, enter "bantam" as a keyword, and locate the correct Web site in less than a minute. If Bantam Doubleday Dell did not appear in Open Market's directory, she could expand the search by making use of other tools such as the World Wide Yellow Pages, Yahoo, and Lycos. If none of these searches generated the address for a Bantam Doubleday Dell homepage, Sharon could safely conclude that Bantam Doubleday Dell is not currently maintaining a Web site.

You would be hard pressed to find the answer to this question using traditional reference tools. A long distance phone call to Bantam Doubleday Dell might help, although it is likely that only a few people in the organization know much about the existence or lack thereof of a company Web site. For this question, Internet reference tools are clearly the right choice.

Example Three

Pat is planning a trip to Australia and would like to know what procedures to follow in order to obtain a travel visa. She is also interested in general information about Australia that might be useful in planning her trip.

The best way for Pat to answer this question would be through a combination of traditional and Internet reference tools. A phone call to the Australian embassy in Washington, D.C. (using a governmental directory to find the phone number) should elicit the procedural information for obtaining a visa. A search of the Yahoo index for Australian sites will yield vast amounts of relevant information for the prospective tourist.

A ROSE IS A ROSE IS A . . . OR IS IT?: PRINT V. INTERNET VERSIONS OF REFERENCE RESOURCES

When we think about reference tools, some types of tools leap to mind immediately. Dictionaries, atlases, and encyclopedias are examples of canonical reference tools. Sites that use the names of each of these tools exist on the Internet. But to use an online dictionary, atlas, or encyclopedia is not necessarily similar to using the print equivalents of any of those tools. Note that I'm not speaking here of the for-fee Internet-accessible interfaces for commercial reference tools like the McGraw-Hill Encyclopedia of Science and Technology or Britannica Online, but rather of free tools established for the Internet community.

Let's look a bit more closely at an example of each of the three types of tools I've mentioned. All three of my examples are available in the General Reference section of the Internet Public Library's Ready Reference Collection.

First, let's investigate an online dictionary. Tyler Jones maintains a Spanish-English dictionary at

http://www.willamette.edu/~tjones/forms/span2eng.html.

His description of the dictionary is extremely straightforward: "This is a very small Spanish dictionary, with a very simple interface . . . The dictionary contains approximately 1300 terms."

This dictionary would be most useful if you needed a basic definition for a relatively common Spanish word whose meaning you had forgotten. For instance, if you search the word "pollo," the dictionary returns with "el pollo: chicken" extremely quickly. But you would not want to use this dictionary if you were searching for uncommon words, or doing anything for which you would need pronunciation, etymology, or any other more complex lexicographic information.

The University of Virginia maintains the Virginia Online Atlas at

http://ptolemy.gis.virginia.edu:1080/tigermap.html.

The atlas generates maps of any Virginia county or independent city based on criteria that the user enters in a forms interface. So it would be extraordinarily useful if you wanted to isolate a particular feature, like pri-

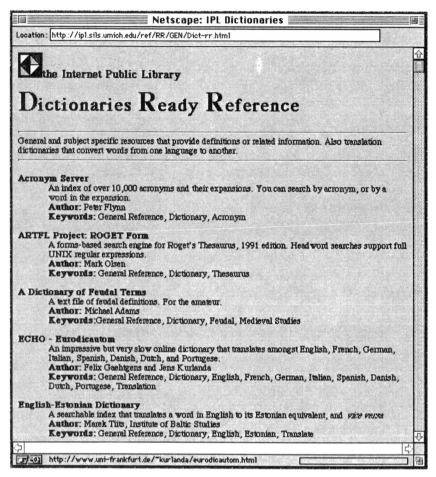

Figure 2–1   Online Dictionaries in the Internet Public Library

mary roads, in a number of counties. However, the atlas is based on data from 1992, so if there had been a lot of construction in your county between 1992 and this year, the generated atlas would not be as accurate as you could wish. This is not really an Internet resource problem, however—all libraries deal with the problem of maintaining currency in their reference resources. The other obvious limitation of this resource—that its coverage is only of the state of Virginia—is not an Internet resource problem either, but rather simply an issue of the scope of the resource. So in this case, an online atlas actually does not differ substantially from its print counterpart, and in fact may be more useful in certain circumstances, because it can generate maps with the particular combinations of features in which you are interested.

Kevin Lowey maintains a site called Kevin's Internet Encyclopedia at http://duke.usask.ca/~lowey/encyclopedia/.

Kevin Lowey's site resembles a print encyclopedia in that the other pages he references are organized into "volumes" in alphabetical order. However, where in a print encyclopedia you would expect to find an extensive article defining and discussing each topic, there is instead only a short definition, followed by a list of links to sites that treat the topic in some fashion. This would be quite useful if you were searching simply for a collection of sites treating a particular topic, but if you were trying to find a comprehensive treatment of the topic, you would be better off searching a print encyclopedia.

Kevin's Internet Encyclopedia also serves to highlight a significant tendency of Internet resources. Kevin says in his introduction, "This is a personal project of mine, and not a service of the University of Saskatchewan." Many Internet resources exist simply because various individuals decided to make a particular set of information available. The level of accuracy and comprehensiveness of these resources is entirely dependent upon the individuals that maintain them.

You now have at least a little bit of an idea of the types of questions that are appropriate to be answered via the Internet, and of the potential differences between print and electronic versions of similarly named tools. However, the most important part of the search process is not simply realizing that you might want to answer a question using the Internet, but knowing where to look once you're there.

KNOWING WHAT TO LOOK FOR

We are far from being able to catalog the Internet, despite the claims of the Lycos search engine, which refers to itself as the "Catalog of the Internet." But it *is* possible to define some types of information that you are likely to find on the Internet, and other types that you are not likely to find. It will help your search process immensely to have some idea of the probability that the information you're seeking actually exists on the Internet.

Types of Information Likely to be Found on the Internet

- First, an obvious one. You will have little trouble finding anything relating to **computers and the people who use them**: hardware and software specifications, programming language manuals and tutorials, computer humor, product and price information from companies, et cetera. Remember that the "computer people" were around on the Internet before anyone else discovered it. They've been helping each other and arguing with each other since before some of the folks who are now surfing the Web were born.

- And, along the same lines: **scientific and technical information**. Scientists have been using the Internet for years and years as well. Any college or university that deals with science and engineering will maintain departmental information, which will frequently include discussions of current research. Professors and graduate students make abstracts and, more rarely, the full texts of their papers available. There is also no shortage of utilities for unit conversion, tables of fundamental physical constants, and other resources of use to people in scientific and technical fields.

- **Popular culture and entertainment**. If someone loved it while they were growing up, or can't go a Tuesday night without watching it now, there's information about it on the Internet. Television shows and movies are reviewed, comic books and toys are idolized and sold, stars are idolized and/or hated—and in either case, their pictures are scanned. (Parenthetically, if you think about what you would get if you combined the three types of information I've just outlined, you will understand very quickly why the Internet is the largest repository of information about **science fiction** in the known universe.)

- **Opinions**. I'm not being facetious. The Internet is, among many other things, a vast conglomeration of opinions, some informed, some uninformed. Survey researchers are just beginning to use those opinions seriously to study the populations on the Internet. But obviously, having access to a huge number of wildly divergent opinions about any given subject is both a blessing and a curse for the information seeker.

- **PR-type Company Information**. You constantly hear about businesses coming online, and how developing a Web presence is of increasing importance in today's business climate. Thus you might expect that you could find substantive information about companies on the Internet. Sometimes you can. But you are far more likely to find a site that describes why Company X is the best possible company in the whole world for producing widgets, than to find a site that contains the complete product specifications and the prices of all currently manufactured widgets.

Types of Information Less Likely to be Found on the Internet

- **Historical information,** particularly information that is at all obscure and/or detailed. There are sites that treat major historical figures and events, of course, but if you're trying to find out anything about, say, the details of a seventeenth century peasant rebellion in Wales, you're probably not going to find it on the Internet. Unless, of course, the preeminent researcher on the topic has decided to make her research available, which is always a possibility, but not a high probability.

- **Humanities information** in general. There are more and more humanities sites appearing all the time, but the amount of humanities information available doesn't come close to approaching the amount of information that's available for scientists. Part of the reason for this is that humanities scholars do not necessarily "need" the computer the way scientists and engineers do, although, as an example, the ability to perform complex and minutely detailed searching within scholarly texts has had a major influence on recent linguistics research.

- And I'll end with another obvious one: **proprietary information**. Companies that have been charging for access to their information for years and years aren't going to be struck suddenly with a burst of altruism to share their data with J. Random Surfer. This is not to say that you won't be able to find a gateway *to* the information via the Internet, merely that in order to reach the information itself, you'll have to pay. A good example of this is the Knight-Ridder site at

  http://www.dialog.com/,

  which provides information about Knight-Ridder Information Services (including an extremely useful descriptive listing of all the files available on Dialog) and even a Telnet gateway to search Dialog—but you must be a current subscriber to Dialog to use the gateway, because it requires your Dialog login ID and password.

KNOWING WHERE TO LOOK

We can break down Internet searching into three categories:

- **Finding People**
- **Finding Information**
- **Finding Tools that make it easier to find People and Information**

These three categories do not demand *radically* different search strategies, but they do differ enough to warrant being discussed individually.

Finding People

There are a number of questions to consider when you're thinking about searching for people on the Internet.

- Most broadly, what sort of people are you looking for? Scholars? Businesspeople? Children? Adults? Librarians?
- Are you looking for an individual or a group?
- If you are looking for an individual, is the individual affiliated with any particular organization?
- Are you looking for a specific person, or simply "someone who would know about X"?

The easiest way to find individuals who are affiliated with particular organizations is to search for the organization.

If you know that a scholar has an appointment at the University of Michigan's Department of Electrical Engineering, it is extremely easy to find the department's Web site from the main College of Engineering page

(http://engin.umich.edu/college/)

and look at the list of faculty there to find the scholar in whom you are interested.

If you know that a programmer is working for Netscape Communications Corporation, it is equally easy to find the list of "Netscape People" from Netscape's main page

(http://home.netscape.com/)

and locate her.

To search for an individual whose institutional affiliation you are unaware of is only slightly less straightforward, though your ability to find the person is entirely dependent on whether or not they want to be found.

Think of it as though you were trying to find someone's phone number when the *default* is that all phone numbers are unlisted, unless the person calls the telephone company and requests that they be included in the telephone directory. In order to be discoverable on the Internet, a person must register themselves with one or more of the available directory services.

One of the more popular directory services available is the Four11 White Pages, at

http://www.four11.com/,

which (like a growing number of Web services) has both a free and a for-fee interface.

Each person's directory entry in Four11 contains a number of fields, from the standard (name and affiliation) to the less common (favorite authors, favorite IRC channels, former high school), to facilitate searching. So if you were trying to find your old best friend from high school, you could do that using Four11—always assuming that your old best friend had registered with Four11 and listed his high school as part of his directory entry.

If you're simply trying to find a contact person to get more information about "X", and "X" has a presence on the Web, the easiest way to establish that sort of contact is to send e-mail to the webmaster of "X"'s site. The address for the webmaster will almost invariably be webmaster@blah.org, where "blah" is the domain name of the organization.

But suppose you were trying to find a group of people. Suppose you are a rabid Melissa Etheridge fan, and want to find other fans with whom to discuss her music. Nova Southeastern University maintains a searchable database of electronic mailing lists at

http://www.nova.edu/Inter-Links/cgi-bin/lists.

A search on "Melissa Etheridge" would yield more than one discussion list.

Finding online communities will be discussed in more detail in the section about "Online Communities as Tools for Research and Reference."

Finding Information

Let's start by going back to the question asked earlier in this chapter: "How do I find the latest version of the Netscape software?" One way to do this, of course, would be to use one of the Web's search engines to find Netscape's homepage and download the software from there. But let's say that for some reason you can't get to Netscape's page—that, improbable as it may seem, http://home.netscape.com is down, and you need your software today.

You can find several sites from which you can download the Netscape software, or any other freeware or shareware in which you might be interested, by using the ArchiePlex search form at

http://cuiwww.unige.ch/./archieplexform.html

The ArchiePlex search form is a gateway to Archie itself; it searches the archives of anonymous FTP servers around the Internet.

Suppose you'd like to find a picture of a rabbit. The most obvious way to do this would be to use one of the Web search engines such as Lycos, OpenText, or InfoSeek and perform a search on the words "rabbit and gif," because gif is the most common image format supported on the Internet.

These are fairly straightforward methods, and you can extrapolate from them to find other types of software or other types of pictures without too much trouble.

But what if you've got an incredibly strange question—a question that you can't even begin to approach answering, but that somehow seems like something you ought to be able to answer using Internet resources? There's at least one mechanism for this sort of "referral" on the Internet as well. The Internet Public Library,

http://ipl.sils.umich.edu/

maintains a reference question answering service staffed by librarians and library students, as well as a substantial Ready Reference collection. You might wish to search the Ready Reference collection

(http://ipl.sils.umich.edu/ref/RR/)

before you send in your question.

Finding Tools that Make it Easier to Find People and Information

You've got one very good tool for finding people and things in your hands right now—namely, this book. A wide variety of Internet books provide complimentary information. Some evaluate resources in particular subject areas. Others offer a general introduction to finding information on the Internet.

Most sites that concern themselves at all with helping new Internet users to find information contain links to the major search engines and Internet directories. Some sites provide comprehensive lists of available

Figure 2–2   The Internet Searching Center

directories and search engines. For instance, the Clearinghouse for Sub-ject-Oriented Internet Guides has a section called "The Internet Searching Center" which serves as an index to other search tools, while other sites such as the Internet Public Library provide links to fewer tools, but with more detailed evaluation of the coverage of each one.

This may sound paradoxical, but the best way to find search tools is to use search tools. Start with some of the tools described in this book. You will see that tools and directories frequently refer back and forth to each other. If you don't find what you're looking for in your initial search, you can usually find other searching tools referenced on the very page where you performed your initial search. And the more time you spend online using different tools, the better idea you will have of which tools are ap-propriate for which purposes. You will also develop an increasingly accu-rate sense for the sorts of information you will and will not be likely to find on the Internet.

Evaluating Resources

What defines a good Internet reference source? I'll quote from the In-ternet Public Library's collection development policy:

The IPL will seek to collect Internet resources which:

- Are high in useful content, preferably those which provide information in their own right rather than simply providing pathways to information.
- Are updated consistently (unless the nature of the resource is such that updating is unnecessary, e.g. an online bible).
- Are designed so that any graphics are an attractive complement to the information rather than a flashy distraction from it.
- Provide text-only interfaces for non-graphical browsers.
- Show evidence of having been proofread carefully (no spelling/grammatical errors or faulty tagging).

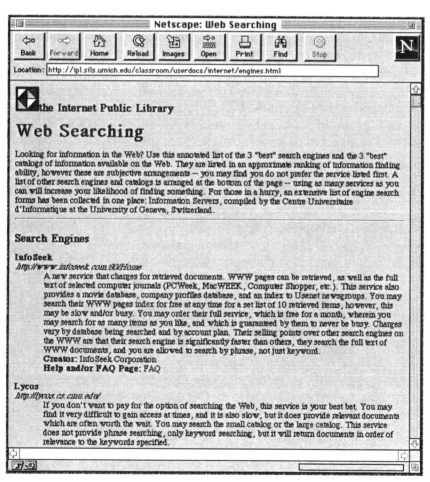

Figure 2–3   The Internet Searching Guide at the IPL

- Contain only "live" links to documents which are as relevant as the primary document.

Some other things to consider when you are evaluating Internet resources are the amount of time it takes to access the resource, the popularity of the site (some sites are so popular that it is difficult to "get through" to them), and the stability of the server on which the resources are stored.

These considerations may be more or less relevant to your particular needs. For instance, if you were designing a reference repository for graphic designers, obviously you would be less concerned about your reference resources providing a text-only interface.

Designing a Personal Reference Site

Many people who are first starting to use the Internet spend an incredible amount of time writing down the addresses of the sites they've found. Then, when they are trying to find the sites again, they first have to remember where they put the piece of paper they wrote the address on. Other people use the Bookmarks feature available in most Web browsers to create placeholders to sites. This feature can be overused. A list of bookmarks can become merely a record of all the sites you've visited. A list of bookmarks cannot convey any sense of whether a particular page is important or was simply something you visited at random. This is not to say that a page you visited at random cannot be important—in fact, serendipity is one of the most important characteristics of spending time on the Internet. You are almost guaranteed to find something that's useful to you professionally in the place where you'd least expect to find it. Of course, you'll also find any number of distracting fun sites when you're trying to find something that's professionally useful.

Eventually, you will probably decide that you would like to have all the information you've been gathering accessible in one place, with a modicum of organization and structure. It would be even nicer if you could access your list via the Web.

What you're thinking about when you think of a list like this is a **hotlist.** You will see many, many hotlists as you spend time on the Internet. The Free Online Dictionary of Computing

(http://wombat.doc.ic.ac.uk/)

defines a hotlist as follows:
"A document on the World Wide Web or a user's browser configuration file containing hypertext links, often unorganized and undocumented, to notable pages on the Web."

A hotlist can be very useful. But its most obvious drawback is that it does not convey any information about the sites referenced other than their titles, which are not always terribly illuminating. A hotlist is really just a Web-accessible version of a Bookmarks file. (In fact, there are many programs which will convert hotlists to HTML format.)

You may decide that you don't need anything more elaborate than a hotlist. If you are using only a relatively small collection of sites, and you know exactly what sort of information each site provides, to write additional text describing each site would be extraneous. However, if your site will serve as a reference not only for you, but for other people you work with or other Net users, you will probably want to create a more detailed site.

There are many, many places you can go on the Internet to learn about composing good HTML, (which you should be able to find using the strategies I've outlined earlier in this chapter) so we won't discuss it here. What we are concerned with is the content of your reference site, not the tags you will use to format it for the Web.

The first thing to think about when you are designing a reference site is your audience. What are the needs of your community?

- Are they novice or sophisticated Internet users?
- Do they have high or low speed connections to the Internet?
- Do they tend to have an easier time using text or graphical user interfaces?

You may want to do some sort of survey of your users to determine the answers to these questions if you don't already have a good sense for the answers. You can think of other questions along these lines.

Once you have established the characteristics of your audience, you can begin thinking about the way you will describe the sites to which you provide links. It is important to work out a consistent scheme for describing your sites. The description could be a simple paragraph explaining what the resource provides. It could be a list of the pros and cons of using this particular resource. It could even be simply an icon from a set of descriptive icons you would define elsewhere on your pages. Look at the organizational structures of sites you admire to get ideas.

If you are going to be collaborating with others in the development of the reference site, it is absolutely essential to develop a style sheet or template for the use of all the developers. The template will ensure that your site has a consistent look and feel, which will make it much easier for your users to navigate. Again, look at the sites you admire and find useful to get ideas.

I can't stress enough that when you're developing your site, you should think about what resources are **useful** to you. Any resource you've used to answer a reference question is probably worth including in a reference site. Also, realize that you will never be able to find all the resources of potential use to you by yourself. Make it possible for users of your site to suggest new resources.

And one bit of advice: don't worry about having your site perfected before you make it available to the public. It will never be perfect. Users of the Internet don't expect perfection. Users will, however, tell you what they think your site is lacking, which will help you to make it better.

Chapter Three

Using the Internet for Research

by Peter Morville, M.I.L.S.
Vice President, Argus Associates
Managing Editor, Clearinghouse for Subject Oriented Internet Resource Guides

INTRODUCTION

To conduct research is to search or investigate carefully and exhaustively. Variations on the definition range from comprehensive academic research within a particular discipline to less structured research on a personal topic of interest. A university professor searching through piles of bibliographies for academic articles about molecular engineering is conducting research. So is the hobbyist trying to compile a list of model railroad clubs, conferences, and events around the country.

Although many of the same search tools are useful in conducting ad hoc or reference queries, the goals and processes of research are very different. The goal of an ad hoc query is to find the answer to a specific question. The goal of a research investigation is to find all or most of the information on a particular topic. Reference queries are usually short and simple. Research queries tend to extend over days, weeks, or months, be highly iterative and interactive, and involve a wide range of tools and resources. Traditional research tools include library catalogs, reference books, microfilms, CD-ROMs, commercial online databases, and the telephone. Some tools are relatively new while others have been around for hundreds of years.

Some would have us believe that the global Internet is the ultimate research tool. Digital libraries, electronic journals, image databases, and hypermedia encyclopedias put information from around the world at our fingertips. Intelligent agents scour the networks searching for new information to index. Powerful search engines with well designed query interfaces provide intellectual access to this vast ocean of knowledge.

This dream of an Internet information utopia that provides one stop shopping for professional researchers and amateur hobbyists alike is a long way from being realized. The contents of most books, journals, magazines, technical reports, and databases are not available via the Internet. In fact, when compared with the volume of information available in print, the Internet's vast oceans seem more like lakes or puddles. Today's Internet is a distributed chaotic environment that changes every day. The most useful information resources of today may be gone tomorrow. Servers crash and phone lines go down. Resources vary tremendously with respect to quality, currency, and level of organization. There is no editorial board and no enforceable standard for content. Information on the Internet may be out of date, misleading, or just plain wrong. To make things worse, there's no top-down organizational hierarchy and no card catalog to cyberspace. Locating useful information can be as difficult as finding a needle in a haystack.

Despite these problems, the Internet does provide access to a growing body of information that is far less accessible via the traditional research tools. Government publications, product and service information, technical data, software programs, and weather statistics are just some of the information resources that are most easily accessible via the Internet. The distributed and digital nature of the Internet lends itself well to information which changes constantly and must be gathered from multiple locations. Since any individual or organization can make information available, we tend to see great volumes of sales and marketing literature, political commentary, travel advertisements, and so on. The Internet is an information space to which anyone can contribute, and they do. Much of the information is useless but some can be very useful. The skilled researcher learns to make use of the various tools and resources for sifting through this ocean of data for the information they need.

The collection of tools and resources for conducting Internet research is rich and varied. Virtual libraries, Internet directories, search tools, and communities of people are all available to help in the search. Some of the search tools such as Lycos and Open Text are highly automated, employing intelligent software agents and powerful search engines. Others such as the Clearinghouse and the World Wide Web Virtual Library integrate human effort and software tools to provide topical access to information resources. None of these tools provides a complete solution. In order to search or investigate carefully, the researcher must integrate a number of complimentary tools. Internet resource discovery is an iterative and interactive process in which a searcher makes use of virtual libraries, directories, search tools and communities of people to find Internet information resources. An Internet directory might lead to an online community where someone mentions an electronic journal which points to a virtual library, and so on. It's important to keep in mind that Internet resource discovery is more an art than a science. The Internet's chaotic and ever changing nature will ensure that some of the tools and resources described in this book will be replaced over the coming months and years. However, the basic principles and heuristics of conducting Internet research described here should endure as the environment evolves.

THE RESEARCH PROCESS

Perhaps the best way to illustrate the iterative and interactive nature of Internet research is to lead you through a sample guide building project from beginning to end. For the purposes of this section, imagine that Susan, a librarian at the University of Athens has been contacted by John, a professor in her university's biology department. The professor is interested in exploring the potential for incorporation of Internet resources into his environmental studies curriculum. After some discussion, Susan and John decide that a topical guide to environmental resources on the Internet might be the best way to introduce the students to the Internet. Susan will develop the guide and John will provide assistance where necessary.

Selecting a Topic

Selecting a specific topic for the guide is the first step. Environmental studies is a very broad area and it's likely that one or more guides on the topic already exist. Susan decides to conduct a preliminary survey of existing guides in this area. There are two primary Web sites where such topical guides are collected. Susan first checks the Clearinghouse for Subject Oriented Internet Resource Guides where she finds several guides to environment related resources.

She then checks the World Wide Web Virtual Library where she finds a couple more guides. Susan summarizes the contents of each guide and then meets with John to discuss how to proceed. They discuss the possibility of simply using one of the existing guides for the course. However, none of the existing guides has the right type of focus or approach. They choose to focus their guide on ecology, the branch of science concerned

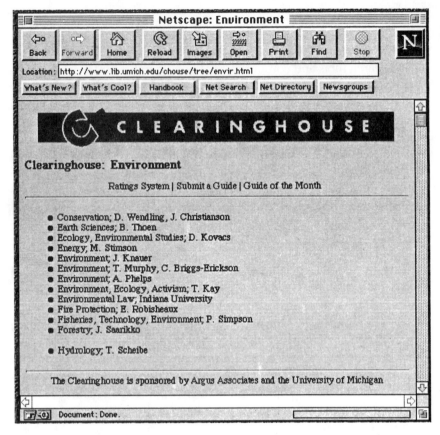

Figure 3–1   Environment Section of the Clearinghouse

with the interrelationship of organisms and their environment. John provides Susan with some background material on the field and explains the types of information that would be most useful to his students. He also provides a list of related keywords such as ecosystem, biodiversity, symbiosis, and preservation. Having selected the topic, Susan is ready to start the research.

Virtual Libraries

Virtual libraries or value-added collections of Internet resources are a great place to begin. The primary strength of virtual libraries arises from the fact that real live people (sometimes called "cybrarians") have added value to these collections through the identification, selection, description, evaluation, and organization of resources. Essentially, these cybrarians create subject-oriented guides or Web sites for use by the Internet community. Topics that are covered in virtual libraries are often covered in great depth. Additionally, the resources are often pre-selected and well organized. On the down side, virtual libraries do not tend to be comprehensive in their coverage of topics and the currency of resources depends upon the busy schedules of the people who maintain them. Virtual libraries are typically organized by topic. Users browse through the hierarchical subject trees from level to level. Some provide search capabilities but browsing is the primary means of navigation.

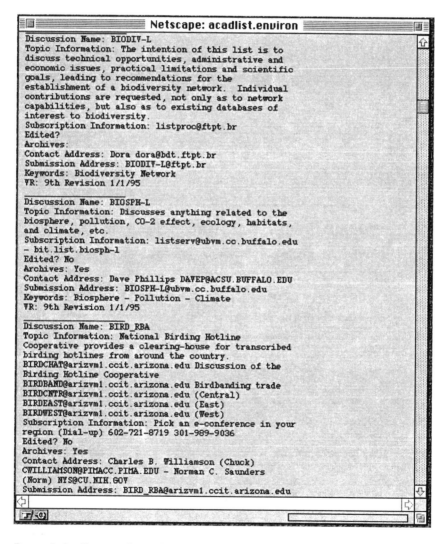

Figure 3–2   Excerpt from the Guide to Ecology and Environmental Studies by Diane Kovacs

A good virtual library to begin with is the Clearinghouse, where Susan already conducted her preliminary survey. She returns to the Clearinghouse and selects "Environment" from the main topic menu. This leads her to a collection of guides on topics such as conservation, earth sciences, ecology, the environment, and environmental law. Susan selects the guide to ecology and begins to browse through the resource descriptions.

This guide focuses solely on Usenet newsgroups and electronic mailing lists that relate to the topics of ecology and environmental studies. Susan reads through the descriptions and makes note of the subscription

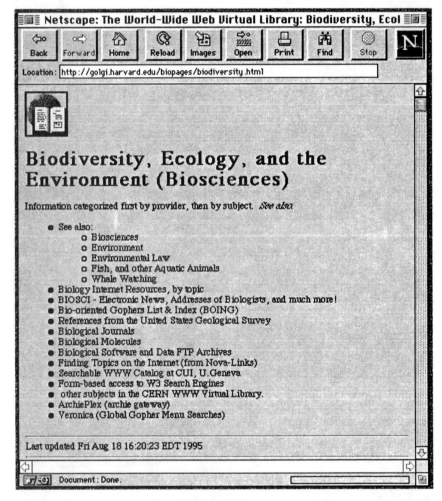

Figure 3–3   Biodiversity, Ecology, and the Environment in the World Wide Web Virtual Library

information for the discussion groups that look to be both pertinent and interesting. Susan then moves on to visit the World Wide Web Virtual Library and GNN's Whole Internet Catalog (WIC). Of the three, the WWW Virtual Library is the broadest in terms of scope, with a huge subject tree. However, some of the topic areas are sparse in coverage; the quality varies substantially from area to area. Susan selects "environment" from the top level categories and then "biodiversity and ecology" from the sub-categories. She then browses through the several dozen resource listings. Some brief descriptions are provided, but for the most part this listing consists of just hyperlinked titles.

The WIC is at the other end of the spectrum with a well organized collection of only the best resources in each topic. Rather than attempting to be comprehensive, the WIC focuses on selection, organization, and description. Informative descriptions are provided for each resource.

Susan browses through the WIC, follows links which look interesting, and takes notes on the potentially useful resources that she finds.

Internet Directories

Susan then decides to visit an Internet directory or collection of resources maintained by the global Internet community. With several million po-

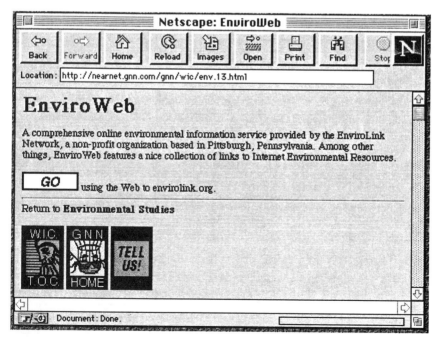

Figure 3–4   A Sample Resource Description from the Whole Internet Catalog

tential contributors, the strength of Internet directories clearly lies in their ability to be relatively comprehensive and current. The primary disadvantage lies in the lack of editorial control over content and organization. Within limits, anyone can add any information to these directories, so the quality varies widely. Coverage tends to be broad rather than deep. You can find information on almost any topic, but not a lot of information on each topic. Directories typically provide options for browsing and searching. As they grow in depth and breadth, the browsing feature becomes less useful while the searching capabilities become increasingly important. Susan begins with Yahoo, the largest and most popular of the directories. Susan can choose to browse the topical hierarchy or enter a keyword search. She decides to try browsing first and selects "environ-

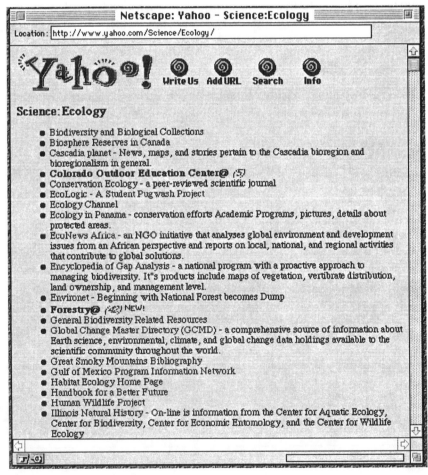

Figure 3–5   The Ecology Section of Yahoo

ment," a sub-category listed under "society and culture." She then selects "ecology" from the menu and browses through a list of over 50 resources.

Some of the resources are of low quality or out of date, but many are very interesting. One of the resources is an extensive list of pointers to ecology-related Web sites. There's no topical organization, but it's useful nonetheless. After reviewing all of the resources, Susan decides to try a keyword search.

Using "ecology" as her keyword, she finds some new resources not located in the ecology category. Most of the new resources are organizations or universities with ecology-related programs. A few are blatant advertisements with no interesting content, but most provide at least some

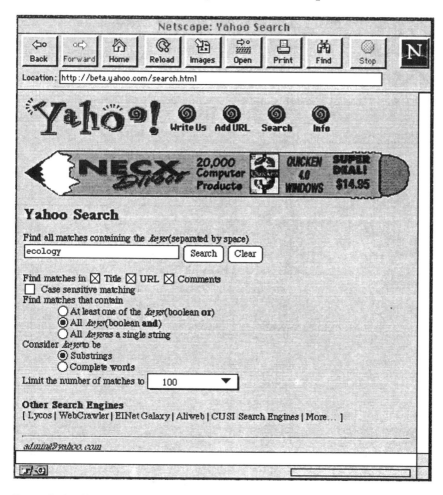

Figure 3–6   Keyword Search Interface for Yahoo

useful information. After Yahoo, Susan moves on to try a few of the other Internet directories. She finds significant overlap but also some new resources.

Search Tools for Finding Information, Software, and People

Having explored the virtual libraries and Internet directories, Susan is ready to employ some of the Internet search tools. Search tools constitute the most diverse category of Internet resources. Some permit fielded queries using Boolean logic while others provide only a simple keyword search of full text documents. Search tools may be used to search for information, software, people, or communities of people. The common characteristic shared amongst all of these tools is the provision of keyword searching capabilities in contrast to the emphasis placed on the browsing of hierarchical topic trees that we have seen in the virtual libraries and Internet directories. Susan begins with Lycos, a search tool that provides access to one of the most comprehensive full text indices of Web documents in existence.

Figure 3–7   The Search Interface for Lycos. Copyright 1995 by Lycos, Inc. All rights reserved.

Susan searches the full text of over five million documents using "ecology" as her keyword. Lycos finds almost 5,000 matching documents and displays the first ten. The hits are ranked in order of "relevance" according to a ranking algorithm. Documents with most references to the keyword, particularly near the beginning of the document are ranked highest. While these relevance ranking algorithms are far from perfect, Susan feels comfortable assuming that the top ranked documents will tend to be most useful. She decides to review the first 50 or so documents and then move on to a more specific search. Some of the resources were already discovered during the library and directory searches, but many are new. Quality, currency, and type of content varies widely, but Susan finds some very useful resources using Lycos. Rather than continue searching through 5,000 hits, Susan tries to narrow her search. She uses the keywords "ecology, biodiversity, symbiosis, and preservation" and enters three as the minimum number of matching terms needed for a "hit."

This substantially reduces the number of hits while improving the relevancy of the result set. While scanning through the list of hits, Susan

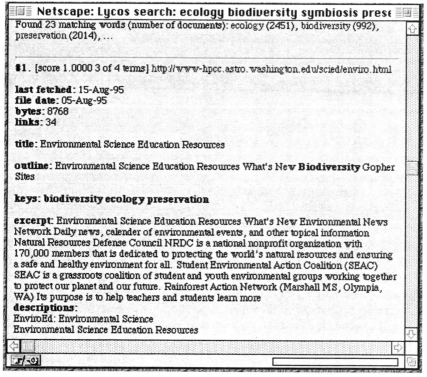

Figure 3–8   Results of a Lycos Query. Copyright 1995 by Lycos, Inc. All rights reserved.

finds a pointer to a software package for modeling ecological processes. This type of software could be very useful for the biology students, so she decides to try a more directed search for software.

Though a member of the previous generation of Internet tools, Archie is still the best tool for finding free software. Archie permits users to search the file names of software packages stored on anonymous FTP servers all around the world.

The problem with Archie lies in the lack of useful information provided in file names. It's easy to find files with names such as "ecology.zip" but names like "eco11.hqx" and "bioec5.exe" make searching more difficult. These difficulties are compounded by the slowness of Archie searches which typically take several minutes. Susan takes advantage of the case

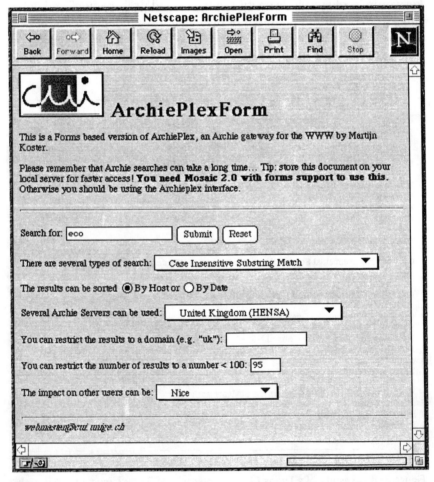

Figure 3–9   Archie: A Frustrating But Useful Tool for Finding Software

insensitive substring matching option. If her keywords show up as any part of a file title, a match will be made. She uses partial words such as "eco" and "bio" and "envir." It takes a while but eventually she finds some very interesting and useful software.

Susan then moves on to use some of the tools for finding communities of people. She already has a list of Usenet newsgroups and e-mail discussion groups that she found in the Clearinghouse, but she'd like to search for more. Using a tool called Publicly Accessible Mailing Lists (PAML), Susan finds a number of e-mail discussion groups on the topic of ecology.

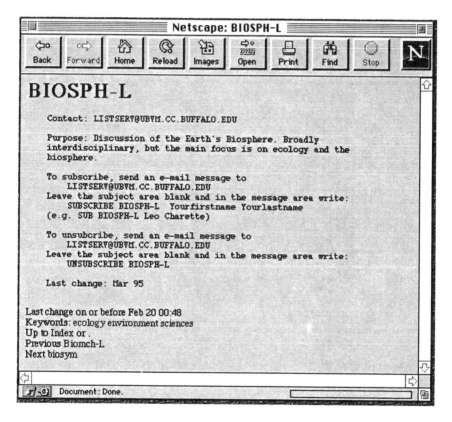

Figure 3–10   Results of a PAML Search

PAML provides brief descriptions of the groups as well as information about how to subscribe and participate. Susan then uses a tool called DejaNews to search through an immense collection of Usenet newsgroups. Results are presented as a list of postings with the name of the newsgroup and the person who submitted the posting.

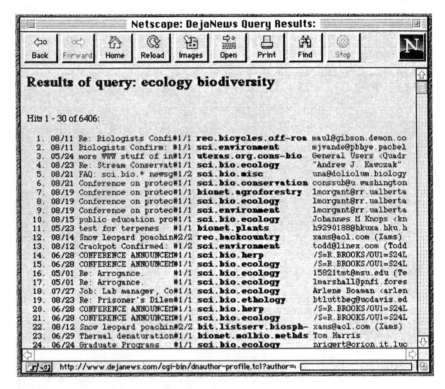

Figure 3–11   Results of a DejaNews Search

DejaNews helps her to find some interesting groups including "sci.bio.ecology" and "sci.environment." Susan starts to monitor each of these groups using her Usenet news reader to get a sense of the volume and quality of the postings.

Susan has now completed the initial research phase of her guide building process. She has browsed through virtual libraries and Internet directories, employed the keyword querying capabilities of search tools, and identified interesting online communities of people. She's now ready to turn her attention toward the development of her guide to ecology related resources on the Internet.

Steps for Conducting Internet Research

- define your topic
- develop a list of related terms
- start with virtual libraries
- explore global information directories
- use Internet search tools
- enlist help from online communities
- follow your leads
- take good notes

DEVELOPING AN INTERNET RESOURCE GUIDE

What is an Internet Resource Guide?

One way that librarians, information professionals, and subject experts are adding value to the networked information environment is through the development of subject-oriented Internet resource guides. For each guide, an author (or team of authors) scours the Internet for information on a particular topic and selects appropriate resources for inclusion. The author then organizes the information according to topic and/or format. Geographical and chronological organization schemes are also used when appropriate. The author may provide descriptive and evaluative information in addition to instructions for accessing the resources.

Over 300 of these guides covering such diverse topics as children's literature, aerospace engineering, computer mediated communication, and environmental law are collected in the Clearinghouse for Subject-Oriented Internet Resource Guides. Founded by Louis Rosenfeld while he was a librarian at the University of Michigan, the Clearinghouse has become a tremendously popular resource. Obviously there is a very real need in this environment for the types of value-added work that librarians and information professionals are well-suited to perform.

People from all around the world develop these topical guides for a variety of reasons. First of all, when conducting Internet research for any reason it's very important to take good notes on where you go and what you find. In order to make this growing collection of notes more manageable, it helps to organize the information by topic or format, add descrip-

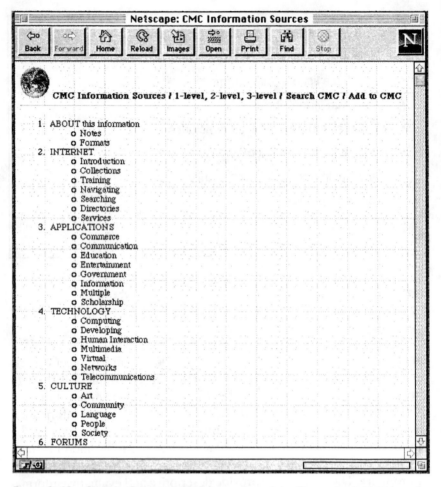

Figure 3–12   Sample Organization Scheme from John December's Guide to the Internet and Computer Mediated Communication

tions, and format the references to each resource in a standard manner. Pretty soon your personal note taking evolves into a well structured and fairly comprehensive guide to resources on your topic of interest. Why not make this guide available via the Internet so that others can benefit from your hard work? It's a great service to the Internet community and you might even get a little famous within your field or area of interest.

Some librarians and subject specialists decide to make a guide available to their patrons via the Internet as an extension of their traditional collection development efforts. Others, like Susan, may work with a faculty member to design a guide around a college course, and then use that guide as a resource for teaching students how to use the Internet for

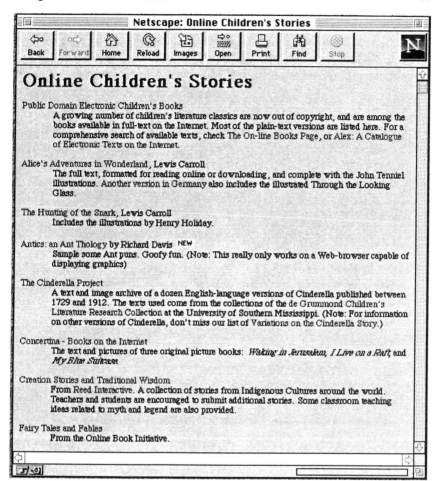

Figure 3–13 Resource Descriptions in Children's Literature Web Guide by David Brown

research. Information professionals in corporate settings may develop a guide to useful resources for their sales or marketing or research departments. Alternatively, an organization may sponsor development of a guide that is designed to attract potential customers to their World Wide Web site. Whatever the reason, the development of a subject-oriented guide is an integral part of conducting Internet research.

Armed with dozens or even hundreds of resources, Susan is ready to begin developing her Internet resource guide. But make no mistake; there's still much work to be done. The process of transforming a raw list of resources into a well developed guide is both time consuming and intellectually challenging. But it makes all the difference in the world.

Through the selection, description, evaluation, and organization of resources, a guide author shapes chaos into order. The resulting guide is a value-added information product that can really help people to find the information they need.

The Design Process

When designing an Internet resource guide, it's important to balance form and function. Before Mosaic and Netscape arrived on the scene, developers were limited to the plain text world of Gophers and ASCII guides. Without the distraction of graphics, developers concentrated solely on

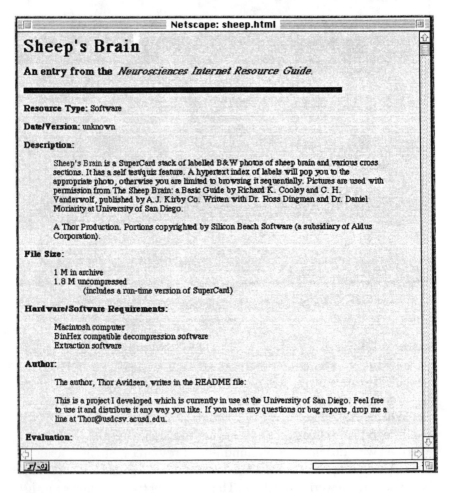

Figure 3–14   A Sample Resource Description from the Neuroscience Internet Resource Guide: The limited use of graphics combined with well-organized textual elements creates a useful and asthetically pleasing page.

functionality. However, on today's World Wide Web the graphical capability often gets in the way. Too many developers go for the flashy high impact graphics that take forever and a day to load. While aesthetics are important, primary consideration should be given to the usability of the guide. A modest graphic on the main page combined with a smaller graphic on all subsequent pages is usually sufficient.

Several factors contribute to the usability of a guide. First of all, the foundation of a good guide is built upon the quality of the resource entries. Information about each resource should be presented in a consistent manner. Begin with meta-information or details about the resource. What is the title? How about the URL? Provide some keywords to suggest the content. Who maintains the resource? In addition to meta-information, descriptive and evaluative information are very useful. Users need to know the subject matter of the resource, the intended audience, the quality and currency, the format, and how to access the information. The integration of hypertext links leading directly to the resources themselves is a big help to the user.

Having developed the information about each resource, it's time for Susan to design the template for her resource pages. In order to avoid long pages that are slow to load, it's best to put each resource description on its own page. A nice page layout allows users to scan the meta information, descriptions, and evaluations quickly. Try to avoid forcing the user to scroll down the page to find important information. Consider employing navigational aids such as "back to the main page" links so that users can move around easily and efficiently. It's very easy to get lost when exploring hypertextual documents. Navigational aids can provide the context necessary to maintain a sense of place.

With the individual pages taken care of, Susan turns her efforts to the architectural design of the guide. The most important architectural decision relates to the use of organization schemes. A topical organization scheme is almost always called for, but don't stop there. Organizing the resources by format can also be very useful. A user may only be looking for software programs, journals, or discussion groups. Certain topic areas lend themselves to chronological or geographical organization.

One of the nicest qualities of hypertext is that it supports multiple pathways to the same information. Susan begins with a topical organization scheme. She reviews the resources that she's collected, and begins to sort them into logical categories. Coming up with those categories is not always so easy. Looking at the way others have organized similar resources can often be helpful. A white board or set of index cards can be a useful tool in facilitating this iterative process. When developing organizational

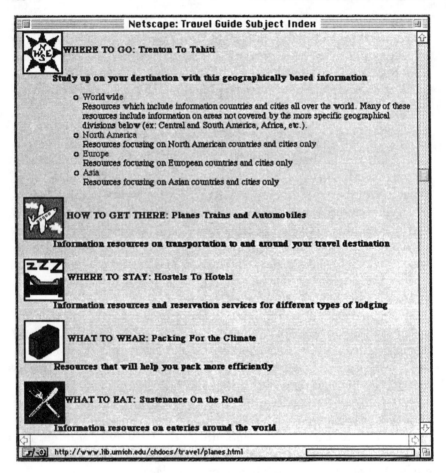

Figure 3-15   Topical and Geographical Organization in the Student and Budget Travel Guide

schemes, key questions relate to the breadth and depth. How many categories should there be? How many sub-categories? How many levels in the hierarchy? Well, there are no definitive answers to these questions, but human-computer interface studies have suggested that menus should include no more than 12 categories (breadth) and hierarchies should have no more than three levels (depth). As hierarchies go beyond these limits, it becomes increasingly difficult for users to find what they're looking for.

Yahoo provides an example of an organizational hierarchy that has grown too broad and deep. A search for ecology-related resources involves navigating through four hierarchical levels with over 75 topics to choose from. It's difficult to find what you're looking for and easy to get lost. In essence, Yahoo's hierarchy is collapsing under its own weight.

Yahoo's Organizational Hierarchy

Yahoo–Top Level

Arts, Business & Economy, Computers & Internet, Education, Entertainment, Government, Health, News, Recreation, Reference, Regional, Science, Social Science, **Society & Culture**

Society & Culture–Level 2

Abortion Issues, Age, Alternative, Animal Rights, Birth, Charity, Children, Civil Rights, Crime, Cultures, Cyberculture, Death, Disabilities, Diversity, **Environment & Nature**, Etiquette, Families, Folklore, Friendship, Gay, Lesbian, & Bisexual Resources, Gender–Transgendered, Gender Issues, Holidays, Homelessness, Human Rights, Hunger, Magazines, Minorities, Museums & Exhibits, Organizations, People, Relationships, Religion, Reunions, Seniors, Sexuality, Singles, Size Issues, Social Work, Veterans, Wedding, Indices

Environment & Nature–Level 3

Alternative Energy, Animal Rights, Business, CIESIN, Companies, Conferences, Conservation, Countries, Databases, Disasters, Discussion Groups, **Ecology**, Education, Environmental Ethics, Environmental Interest Groups, Events, Exhibits, Forestry, Health, Institutes, Law, Mountain Ranges, Oceanography, Online Resources, Organizations, Ozone Depletion, Parks, Pollution, Preservation, Products & Services, Programs, Projects, Public Interest Groups, Publications, Recycling, River, Ocean & Other Water Resources, Sustainable Development, Weather, Wildlife, Indices

Ecology–Level 4

A listing of ecology-related resources. Brief descriptions are provided for some resources.

Figure 3–16. Yahoo's organizational hierarchy is collapsing under its own weight. Just getting to the menu for ecology related resources requires navigating to a level four menu.

One way to balance the growth of organizational hierarchies is to employ search capabilities. At the simplest level, consider using a full text indexing tool to provide keyword access to your information resource pages. Full text indexing is easy to implement and manage and provides the user with a quick way to access information. Even better, consider providing fielded searching capabilities. This way a user can search the author, keyword, description, or evaluation fields. Either way, a query interface can complement organizational hierarchies quite nicely.

Publicity, Feedback, and Redesign

By following some basic principles of design, Susan has developed a useful and usable guide. However, she needs to complete one more step in the process before being ready to turn the guide over to the biology students. Susan should now publicize her guide to some of the Internet communities it covers. People in those communities will probably be very appreciative of her efforts. They are also the best source for feedback on the guide. Susan posts messages to each community announcing the rough draft of her guide. She asks people to take a look and let her know what they think. Before long, Susan starts to receive responses. Some tell her of useful resources which she has missed. Others provide suggestions for enhancing the overall design of the guide. Still others simply thank her for developing such a useful resource. Susan saves the latter messages, incorporates the suggestions, and announces the finished version of the guide. In addition to posting messages to the ecology-related communities on the Internet, Susan submits her guide for inclusion in a number of Internet directories and virtual libraries. She also submits it for indexing by several of the major search tools. Now the guide will be available not only to the biology students at her university but to anyone interested in ecology anywhere in the Internet community.

CONCLUSION

Susan's research project illuminates the iterative and interactive nature of Internet research. It began with the use of virtual libraries, Internet directories, search tools, and online communities of people, and culminated in the development of a subject-oriented guide. No single tool or type of tool could have helped her to identify all of the resources she found during her search. By finding clues and following up on leads, Susan collected a substantial variety of resources. By selecting, describing, organizing, and evaluating resources from that collection, Susan developed a useful guide. Finally, by publicizing the availability of her guide to appropriate communities, Susan made it more readily accessible. However, Susan's work does not end here. The rapid pace of change on the Internet ensures that guides quickly become obsolete without constant updates. Some resources will disappear and new ones will take their place. New formats incorporating interactive video and virtual reality technology will become increasingly prevalent. Old formats will slide into obscurity.

The same will happen with the tools for conducting Internet research. Most of the tools covered in this book did not exist two years ago. How many of today's tools will exist two years from now? What types of advanced tools will take their place? It's impossible to predict all of the twists and turns to come, but certain developments seem inevitable. The quantity of Internet information will continue to grow exponentially. The tools will become more powerful and sophisticated. Humans will continue to play an important role in the identification, selection, description, evaluation, and organization of information. And the process of conducting research via the Internet will remain challenging, interesting, and rewarding.

Chapter Four

Online Communities as Tools for Research and Reference

by Louis B. Rosenfeld, M.I.L.S.
President, Argus Associates
Director, Clearinghouse for Subject Oriented
Internet Resource Guides

COMMUNITIES IN GENERAL: A TWO-WAY STREET

One reason that communities get started is because some individuals discover that they share something in common, such as geography or a mutual interest. But that's only part of the picture. A community is kind of like a bank: members make withdrawals, but also have to leave deposits as well. For example, if you wish to be a part of a community centered around a neighborhood, you'll enjoy a number of benefits, such as familiar faces to greet as you walk down the street, or someone to feed your cat when you go on vacation. But you'll also find yourself mowing an elderly neighbor's lawn or keeping a watchful eye on the local kids playing in the neighborhood. So belonging to a community requires give and take.

Online communities are wonderful, perhaps unequaled information sources. On the other hand, they're often as inconsistent and undependable as are people themselves. The best approach to leveraging the expertise of an online community is to demonstrate your willingness to contribute as well as receive information. This chapter will explain why this is the case; it will also familiarize you with the basics of online communities and how you can use them as sources of information.

THE ONLINE COMMUNITY

An online community is a group of individuals who share and exchange communications regarding a common interest by using information technology. The community can range in size from two people to thousands. Their communications are generally one-to-many; in other words, when an individual communicates, all other members of that community receive or can access that communication. Online communities, unlike most physical ones, are centered around topics rather than geographic locales. The community's shared interest can range from alternative medicine to Yiddish theater to the merits of living in San Francisco; in effect, any topic that is of interest to more than one person on the planet. And there are a number of information technologies that are used to support communities; the most popular are the various programs that support electronic mailing lists (popularly known as "listservs") and Usenet newsgroups, described in the section below titled "Common Tools for Online Communities."

WHY USE ONLINE COMMUNITIES?

This book describes many resources for searching besides online communities: virtual libraries, directories, and indices. All are valuable in some situations, less so in others; none are particularly adept at handling all information needs. Online communities are obviously a bit different than these other resources, as they require you to interact with other Internet users to gather the information you need. This process of interacting with others is very time-consuming; first you'll need to find an appropriate online community, get to know its culture to some degree, and then ask your question. Maybe you'll get some answers right away, maybe you'll get none at all. Perhaps some answers will need clarification, which will add a few more iterations to the process. Considering how drawn out this process might become, is it really worth bothering?

And don't forget the trials of (mis)communication: as with any interaction, things can and often do go wrong. You want to make sure that you don't come off the wrong way when you post your question to an online community. And even if you exercise the utmost care in posting your question, the current volume of traffic on the list may reduce the probability of its attracting a response to almost nil.

So why on earth would you use an online community as a source of information? Because humans are without a doubt the best information filters. They can and often will help you in ways that none of the other resources, all of which are automated, ever will. For example, a person is exposed daily to information from so many different sources: newspapers, books, radio, gossipy acquaintances, television, passersby, even dreams. No piece of software can keep up with all these sources, but many of the people you encounter on mailing lists will be able to almost instantaneously summon from these sources a fact or a pointer to help answer your question, no matter how disjointed it might be.

People will be able to understand something about you and the context of your information need. They'll know to give you a different answer if you're a college professor than if you were nine years old. They will also be adept at handling the ambiguity that is inherent in language. Unlike most software programs, people will understand that if you're looking for statistics about a pitcher, you're not talking about something to pour water from. And ultimately, people often enjoy helping each other; if you pose your question the right way, solving it may serve as an interesting and entertaining challenge for members of an online community. We hope this chapter will equip you to better understand online communities and how to ask your question the "right way."

WHEN TO USE ONLINE COMMUNITIES

Online communities aren't appropriate sources for answers to quick, ad hoc questions. If anything, you'll annoy the members of those communities by bugging them with queries that you likely could have answered by spending just a few minutes doing the research yourself. Besides, who's to say they'll get right back to you with an answer quickly? Rely upon online communities when you're truly stuck, when you want to do in-depth and qualitative searching, and when time isn't a major factor. Here are some basic rules-of-thumb to keep in mind when considering querying an online community. Use them when:

- *you're not in a hurry to get an answer*: As mentioned above, it can take a lot of time for you to find an appropriate online community and properly post your question, much less receive an answer.
- *you're completely stuck*: If you can demonstrate to a community that you've tried to answer the question yourself, you'll likely be able to enlist others who see the seriousness of your efforts.
- *you need to do exhaustive research and want to turn over every stone*: You could use every searchable index, virtual library, and directory available, and still not find resources others may already know about. Additionally, you may learn "insider's information"

about relevant resources that are under development and will be available soon.

- *you're hoping to get a good amount of descriptive information on resources*: While your Yahoo search will tell you that there's a wonderful-sounding archive of music lyrics, a person will not only tell you about that resource's scope, but also mention that it hasn't been accessible for the past four months.

- *you're hoping to get a good amount of evaluative information on resources*: Similarly, people will steer you clear of substandard resources and often provide a few words regarding the quality of a resource. If you get enough responses, you'll find that you've in effect conducted an "opinion poll," and comparing the answers might be very informative.

- *the product of your search is intended to serve a broad audience*: If you are eventually going to make the results of your search widely available, announce that along with your question. It makes sense to enlist the eventual beneficiaries of your hard work in the searching process.

WHAT TO LOOK FOR IN AN ONLINE COMMUNITY

Appropriate people and quality information are the hallmarks of the right online community for your needs. It seems that almost every day we hear of a new resource designed to help users search for mailing lists and newsgroups. (See chapter 7 for more details.) Finding relevant online communities is obviously important and necessary, but is only half of the battle. You'll also want to determine which of those communities are actually *appropriate*. Posting to an inappropriate community will simply be a waste of your time and that community's time.

So what's an appropriate community? Ideally, it should fit the following criteria:

- *traffic levels shouldn't be too high*: Your query is competing with all the other queries posted to that community. Will anyone even notice your posting if it's just one of one hundred? Or even thirty? A good rule of thumb is to post to communities which average a dozen postings per day. At the other extreme, some communities are defunct and therefore make no postings. Does it make sense to post to such a group? Surprisingly, yes—there may actually be a fair number of "lurkers" still subscribing; they may be quite happy to help you, because your query may be interesting enough to reinvigorate their community's discussion.

- *the community's topic should be as narrow and specific as possible*:
  Let's say your query has something to do with Welsh history, and
  your choices of online communities include ones that deal with
  Welsh history and British history. While it may be tempting to post
  to both, the British online history community probably has higher
  traffic levels and fewer Welsh history experts than the Welsh history community. And the folks who do happen to subscribe to both
  communities will come across your posting twice, which might annoy some. So at least start by posting to the Welsh community, and
  if you have no luck there, come back to the British community,
  mention your lack of luck with the other group, and ask there.
- *the community should be supportive of questions*: Spend a few days
  "lurking" or listening in on the discussion that goes on in a given
  online community. Do members "flame" (send derogatory or angry messages) the folks asking questions? If they do, it's probably
  not worth bothering to post your question. Do they often mention
  a useful FAQ (a document containing answers to Frequently Asked
  Questions)? If they do, you ought to check that before asking your
  question. Do they seem to favor one type of question over another?
  If so, emulate the former. In general, your common sense will be
  your best guide here.
- *the community should be capable of assisting with questions*: Do
  the answers to other folks' queries seem to be helpful? Do the dis-
  cussants generally seem competent, or do they come off as uninformed or just plain reckless in their answers? You may find that,
  based on the limited searching you have already done, you have
  become *the* expert on your area of interest relative to the folks in
  the online community.

COMMON TOOLS FOR ONLINE COMMUNITIES

If you're new to Internet communities, you'll want to understand a bit
about their underlying technologies and their relative advantages and
disadvantages. Here are a few things you should know regarding the major
tools for using online communities.

Mailing lists and Usenet newsgroups cover a limitless number of topics. Both types of tools are free to "subscribers" and are fairly easy to use;
therefore, it's not surprising how popular they are. You'll find a lot of
variety in both mailing lists and newsgroups: levels of discussion vary from
highly scholarly or serious to completely sophomoric and meaningless;
community spirit can range from suffocatingly warm-and-fuzzy to supportive to indifferent to downright nasty; and traffic volumes may range

from one posting per month to one hundred per day. This wide variety is due to a number of factors, including the nature of the topic, its audience, the age of the mailing list or newsgroup, and whether its postings are "moderated" or controlled by an individual who has been entrusted with this responsibility. Generally, the postings you'll find on mailing lists tend to be informal in tone; questions, answers, group discussions and arguments prevail, although you'll also encounter more officious postings, such as conference announcements and press releases.

Electronic Mailing Lists

- *how they work*: Commonly known as "Listservs," mailing lists are fueled by plain old electronic mail. Mailing list programs maintain lists of subscribers and their e-mail addresses; each mailing list has its own e-mail address, and when someone sends a message to that address, all the subscribers receive a copy of the posting. Although you may not realize that you're interacting with mailing list programs, it's helpful to recognize a few of the popular "brand names": Listserv, Mailserv, Majordomo, and Listproc are all a little different, but basically do the same things. E-mail is used to subscribe and unsubscribe to a mailing list, to customize one's subscription to a mailing list, and to post and receive mailing list postings. Every posting from a mailing list will end up in your electronic mailbox, along with all your other mail. There are about two to three thousand open mailing lists available today.
- *benefits*: Due to their reliance on widely accepted and common electronic mail technologies, mailing lists are easy to use; if you can use e-mail, you can use a mailing list. Because many of the mailing list technologies come directly from academia, participants are more likely to be "serious academics." Therefore, discussion levels are usually a little more serious than those found on Usenet newsgroups, and it's more likely that a mailing list is moderated or filtered. Mailing list software programs generally provide for archiving their postings, so you can often search for information that may have been posted months or years ago.
- *disadvantages*: It can be intrusive to find mail addressed to a group mixed in with the personal mail in your mailbox. It can be really intrusive to find 50 or 100 of these postings in your mailbox some morning, especially if the topic of discussion isn't your cup of tea. As a solution, some mailing lists can be set to combine each day's worth of postings into one long message called a "digest" that gets mailed once daily. However, digests are less interactive and reduce

the timeliness of receiving postings to once per day. The interface and commands for doing anything aside from receiving and making mailing list postings (e.g., searching an archive or setting your subscription to "digest") are quite awkward.

Usenet Newsgroups

- *how they work*: Much like individual mailing lists, each Usenet newsgroup covers a specific topic. Unlike mailing lists, newsgroups require special software, called "newsreaders," to be accessed. So you'll need to actively access Usenet, as opposed to passively receiving e-mailed postings from mailing lists. Newsreaders come in many varieties which are generally geared toward specific computer platforms, including Trumpet for the Windows environment, Nuntius for Macintoshes, and rn, trn, and tin for UNIX computers. Using your newsreader software, you can subscribe to, view, and post to specific newsgroups. When you access a newsgroup, you'll usually first see an index of all the postings submitted since you last checked. You'll be able to select the specific posting you want to read and easily ignore the others. Some newsreaders also allow you to view a related subset of a newsgroup's postings called "threads"; monitoring an individual thread is akin to listening in on one conversation at a cocktail party and ignoring the others in the room. Depending on the policies of your Internet service provider, only the most recent one or two weeks Usenet newsgroups are archived, so if you don't check your news for a period longer than that, you might miss out on some postings.
- *benefits*: Newsreaders allow you to sift through many postings in a single session without cluttering your electronic mailbox. Additionally, threaded newsreaders enable you to keep up with the interesting discussions going on in a newsgroup while easily ignoring the others. It's much easier to determine the topics of newsgroups than with mailing lists, as Usenet follows a fairly standard convention for naming newsgroups.
- *disadvantages*: Using a newsreader requires you to set up, access, and master yet another piece of software, unlike mailing lists (assuming you're already using e-mail software). You'll also find that the levels of traffic and quality of discussion on newsgroups tends to vary more widely than in mailing lists.

HOW TO ASK YOUR QUESTIONS: DO'S AND DON'TS

Perhaps your biggest challenge lies in getting someone to answer your question. If you come off as an Internet "newbie," or as someone with no sense of the culture of the specific online community, you're likely to be ignored. If you don't follow some basic rules of netiquette, you might be laughed at or flamed. And if you don't time your posting well, many members of the online community may never even notice that you submitted a posting. Following are some common sense do's and don'ts to help you avoid some of the pitfalls along the path to successful queries.

- *do keep your message brief*: We live in times of short attention spans; long postings are simply fodder for delete keys.
- *do identify yourself*: Many ignore all postings from anonymous or pseudonymous names. Use your real name, and, if you have a title that's short and not too officious, add that too. If you are a college student, it's not a bad idea to list your institution, but *never* say that you are a student. Many will assume you're looking for homework help.
- *do state where else you are posting your request*: This is good Internet etiquette, allowing readers who may chance upon your posting a second or third time to easily ignore it.
- *do state your goals*: People will be more likely to help you if you give them a little context for your query; if you can, let them know why you're looking for the information, how you'll use it, and who will benefit from it.
- *do tell them what you already know*: It's important to show that you've done at least some of your homework, so some quick and dirty searching before you post is in order. Besides, you don't really want to get 20 responses describing the obvious or popular resources. You want to know about the resources that are hard to find or that aren't up and running just yet.
- *do ask for the addresses of knowledgeable people*: Finding and befriending a few experts out there will make your life much easier. And having a referral ("so-and-so from such-and-such mailing list gave me your name and suggested that I contact you") will go a long way to break down the expert's defenses.
- *don't ever announce that you're a novice in the area*: Doing so will also reduce the likelihood of a response. And if you do receive a response that isn't clear to you, ask the individual poster for clarification, or show the message to a local expert or friend to see if they can offer an explanation.

- *don't use long and silly sigfiles*: You should project a serious image for yourself and your query, so including a large Bart Simpson graphic in your sigfile won't help your cause.
- *don't send your posting out at night, during the weekend, or at the end of the week*: Timing is important, and you want to do anything to prevent your posting from being one of a batch that came in over the weekend or the night before. These batches are less likely to receive as close attention as would a single posting.
- *do be prepared to repeat your request periodically*: Sometimes you simply won't get any responses no matter what you do. Consider making your preliminary results available so that the community can see that you're actually working on it. This will also provide them with another chance to give you feedback.

This last point recalls our initial discussion about the two-way nature of communities. If you are extensively researching a topic, providing a summary of the results of your search can be a great enticement for members of an online community to respond and help you. As they are already Internet users, they understand how difficult it is to find relevant, useful information. If you portray yourself as one willing to do this work, you will find much more interest (and general encouragement) than if you had simply asked a question without offering up your results.

SUMMARY

The Internet is going to continue to grow at an amazing rate for some time to come. This growth will mean two things:

- More and more information will be available on the Internet; therefore, the automated tools for searching (e.g., Lycos, Yahoo, Webcrawler) will become less and less effective at separating the wheat from the chaff.
- Subsequently, more and more queries will be posted to online communities. Your posting will therefore need to stand out as much as possible from the rest.

We hope that this chapter demonstrates the value of the expertise found in online communities, and helps you to formulate queries effective at unlocking that expertise.

Chapter Five

Virtual Libraries

Contents

AN OVERVIEW OF VIRTUAL LIBRARIES

Virtual libraries or "value added collections of Internet resources" are among the more civilized areas of an otherwise chaotic and unruly cyberspace. Although a far cry from the order and stability of traditional libraries, virtual libraries do provide a taste of the value that librarians can add to the Internet through the application of traditional skills in a vastly non-traditional environment. Through the identification, selection, organization, description, and evaluation of Internet information resources, "digital librarians" or "cybrarians" create virtual libraries which help people to find information, software, and communities of people. Virtual libraries typically provide an organizational hierarchy with topical categories for browsing. Some provide a query interface to allow keyword or full text searching. Some virtual libraries are maintained by a single organization, while others are supported through the volunteer efforts of people around the world.

Strengths

Virtual libraries are most useful when conducting research into a particular topic. Whether you're looking for a few interesting gardening resources or initiating a comprehensive search on the topic of neuroscience, virtual libraries are a great place to begin. The strength of virtual libraries derives from the value added approach to information management. The well-designed organizational schemes help people to locate resources on their topic, and the objective descriptions and subjective evaluations help people to make selections from those resources.

Weaknesses

The human role in the development and maintenance of virtual libraries also leads to their primary weakness. Compared with Internet directories, for instance, virtual libraries are relatively limited in the number of topics they cover. Additionally, quality and depth of coverage often varies widely from topic to topic. Finally, virtual libraries cannot compete in the area of currency. With a few exceptions, virtual libraries are almost totally supported by the efforts of volunteers. It is impossible for these people to keep up with the exponential growth of Internet information resources.

Searching Tips

Virtual libraries are best for conducting research but can also be useful for answering reference questions. Whatever the nature of the query, it's usually easiest to begin by browsing through the organizational hierarchy. This is typically the shortest path to a guide or Web site on a given topic. If you don't find anything by browsing, try the search capability. You may find a guide that leads you directly to a useful resource, or a related resource within a guide which then leads you to a useful resource.

Considerations for the Future

We live in an information age with vast oceans of data at our fingertips. Unfortunately, finding useful information can be as difficult as finding a needle in a haystack. Automated search engines and directories can help, but only so much. Human efforts to identify, describe, organize, and evaluate information resources are an essential component of the solution.

To address the limitations of virtual libraries, a number of organizations are exploring an economic model, namely content driven advertising, which provides a financial incentive for the development and maintenance of top quality virtual libraries. Once this model proves itself, we can expect to see dramatic improvements in the scope, depth, currency, and overall quality of virtual libraries.

As the volume of Internet information continues to grow, users will increasingly turn to the value-added virtual libraries for fast and easy access to Internet information resources. The future of virtual libraries holds great promise.

A DEVELOPER'S PERSPECTIVE

by Frederick Zimmerman
Editor and Publisher
The Internet Book and Information Center

Developing and maintaining the Internet Book Information Center (which operates via the WWW Virtual Library on Literature) has posed a number of interesting challenges—conceptual, technical, and spiritual.

I began thinking about setting up an Internet Book Information Center in Fall 1993. The initial idea was simply to provide a clearinghouse for book-related information on the Internet. My initial prototype ran on a desktop Macintosh Gopher server and pointed only to Gopher and FTP resources. (Remember that in June 1993, there were only 130 WWW sites in existence, according to a survey conducted by Matthew S. Gray, then a student at MIT—http://www.netgen.com/info/growth.html).

Unfortunately, not everyone was enthusiastic about the idea of an Internet Book Information Center. My initial announcements of the prototype Gopher service, posted to Usenet newsgroup rec.arts.books, drew replies from a handful of proprietary and vociferous readers who told me that it was inappropriate for me to call myself an Internet Book Information Center, and that I should confine myself to a title like "A Few Book-Related Links on Fred Zimmerman's Personal Gopher." This was the first major spiritual challenge I faced because, to be frank, the unexpected criticism fazed me.

I came very close to following the advice of the nay-sayers and abandoning the idea of setting up an "Internet Book Information Center." Fortunately, I decided to hold true to my initial vision. I wanted a title that would define my project's identity as a clearinghouse and I felt it was reasonable to stake out a significant niche and work over time to do useful things in it. Over the course of time, my judgment has been vindicated. One of the less obvious effects of the WWW technology on the Internet culture is that it has effected a major shift in balance of power between self-appointed Net police (who, alas, thrive on Usenet) and resource creators (who thrive on the Web).

I putzed around with the prototype for about six months, but the project didn't really take off until my wife Cheryl suggested that I see if I could get some space on a Webserver somewhere. I posted a notice to comp.infosystems.www explaining my idea for an Internet Book Information Center. I was thrilled when Jon Magid from SunSite wrote and offered the use of a courtesy account on Sun's demonstration Webserver at the University of North Carolina (http://sunsite.unc.edu/). I didn't know it at the time, but I had made a connection with a great site that would turn out to be a hotbed of excellent and well-known Web development projects such as the WebLouvre and the Elvis Presley Home Page.

The next major technical and conceptual challenge was doing the resource discovery to make the IBIC home page the best available collection of pointers to Internet resources related to books. Throughout IBIC's existence I've kept "books" and, especially, "book-lovers" as a touchstone. That conceptual clarity has been an important element of keeping the project manageable. After a few months, I was successful in putting together a number of "laundry lists" of authors, publishers, and so on that for quite a while were the best such lists available on the Net.

Those lists led to the next major step forward for IBIC. In summer 1994, I wrote to the maintainers of the WWW Virtual Library asking that IBIC be added to the WWW Virtual Library for Arts and Literature (the two categories were then maintained together). They took a look at IBIC and said, "Your Literature list puts ours to shame! Why don't you maintain a separate WWW Virtual Library on Literature?" That put IBIC on the map with a prime location in the "content architecture" of the Web.

A moral for virtual library developers: getting there first is important. IBIC has been operational since March 30, 1994, which makes it positively geriatric in the world of Internet resource discovery. I was both amused and flattered when *Publishers' Weekly* called IBIC "the granddaddy of book-related resources on the Internet" (June 1995).

Another moral: it's important to communicate with other virtual librarians. The two biggest jumps in IBIC's traffic came when IBIC became part of the WWW VL structure, and when the Global Network Navigator decided to point to IBIC as a primary index of book-related resources.

The rapid growth of the Net posed some important challenges for me. For one thing, I found it hard to keep my lists up to date. If you maintain an Internet virtual library, you will receive a significant amount of unsolicited e-mail from people who want their resource to be listed. A lot of the mail is fun and interesting, and it's great to have a built-in system for current awareness of relevant Internet development; but there is a downside. Many times, I became swamped by e-mail announcements of the newest web site from publisher X or author Y. Many such announcements were of interest only to rather narrow or specialized audiences.

In keeping lists up to date, I gave precedence to resources likely to be of broad interest to a large number of people. (Long-time IBIC readers will realize that I have something of a populist taste in fiction). But over time I became increasingly dissatisfied with being in the "laundry list" business, especially as other web sites also began to offer good lists of book-related resources, sometimes (like Yahoo) taking advantage of self-registering and database tracking technology.

Faced with this change, I returned to an important conceptual principle: the Web is distributed. I think one thing I've done quite well with IBIC is that I've risen to the spiritual challenge of accepting that "it doesn't have to be mine to be good." If someone else has a better list, there's no reason to duplicate the effort. A lot of people seem to have trouble putting this principle into practice. I'm constantly amazed to see how many book-related sites maintain their own separate lists of publishers that differ in only minor details.

I did the initial resource discovery for IBIC by hand, but that wouldn't work today. The technological ante has risen. Doing broad topical resource discovery in a world with 15,000 plus Web sites really requires automated search and discovery tools. If I were trying to build a new virtual library today, I'd want to have a programmable "URL-sifter" that can sort and filter raw URL lists generated by tools like Lycos on the basis of criteria such as domain name, keywords, and so on. And the URLs selected really should be put into a Web-accessible database of some sort. I don't have access to that technology at IBIC, so I've responded by making IBIC less of an exercise in "laundry lists" and more a metaguide, like a Baedeker's or even a Paul Theroux travelogue.

This changing emphasis fits with another important finding: people like point of view. My e-mail and my user statistics tell me that people appreciate the opportunity to interact not just with the virtual library, but with the virtual librarian. I try to make IBIC both "high-tech" and "high-touch." For better or for worse, you get *my* take on books and book-related Internet resources.

I believe it is important to document the perspective that motivates your virtual library. For example, I make it clear on the IBIC homepage that I don't have a major business axe to grind. I'm not trying to sell books or corner the market on Internet web services for publishers. I do want to maintain and grow an audience in such a way that this is a satisfying and self-sustaining investment of my time (and if you are an online publisher who'd like to hire me to do just that, please call!)

Make no mistake, maintaining a virtual library is a significant career investment. Many times I have had to ask myself, is this free project worth the time? I like to assess the issue as analytically as possible. IBIC represents hundreds, if not thousands, of hours of effort. In September 1995, there were almost 200 HTML files comprising more than 1.1 MB of text plus HTML that have been "hit" more than 600,000 times in 18 months of operation. That's the equivalent of writing a good-sized book that has been well received by a substantial audience, and I document it that way on my resumé. Interestingly enough, that argument seems to be pretty well received by the employment marketplace. There's no question that maintaining a virtual library has made me more marketable.

But when I get right down to it, the financial argument isn't quite sufficient to justify the effort. For most of us, I suspect, the decision to maintain a virtual library isn't strictly a matter of dollars and cents. There are two primary considerations which have made it worthwhile for me. First, it's given me an opportunity to "pay back" the world of books— which has given me so much—by using the Internet to serve book-lovers. Secondly, maintaining a virtual library is an opportunity to be at the center of an exciting process of growth and development in a field of lifelong interest. It's simply tremendous fun.

CLEARINGHOUSE FOR SUBJECT-ORIENTED INTERNET RESOURCE GUIDES

Meta Information

URL:	http://www.lib.umich.edu/chhome.html
Resource Type:	World Wide Web site
Use:	finding information resources, software, and online communities; primarily useful for research but may help with some reference queries; best for finding a variety of useful resources under a broad heading; most useful for queries that don't require current information
Navigation:	browse subject hierarchy
Scope:	broad with the following top level categories: arts and entertainment, business and employment, education, engineering and technology, environment, government and law, health and medicine, humanities, news and publishing, regional information, science, social sciences and social issues
Volume:	200 topical guides; note that each guide contains dozens or hundreds of resources
Searching Tips:	select a broad category and scan the guide titles
Strengths:	certain topics covered extremely well, excellent organizational schemes
Weaknesses:	sparse coverage of some topics, variable quality from guide to guide, inability to perform global searches
Updates:	new guides and new versions of guides are added once or twice per month; updates to the guides themselves are dependent upon the authors and vary from guide to guide
Questions:	Louis Rosenfeld, lou@argus-inc.com
Submissions:	http://www.lib.umich.edu/docs/submit.html

Figure 5–1   The Clearinghouse for Subject-Oriented Internet Resource Guides

Description

The Clearinghouse is a collection of over 200 subject specific guides which provide intellectual access to thousands of Internet information resources. Topics covered range from philosophy to personal finance to neuroscience. The guides provide objective descriptions and subjective evaluations as well as instructions for accessing the resources. The Clearinghouse collocates guides which are developed and maintained by authors on remote servers all over the world. Currently, the Clearinghouse includes guides in plain text and/or hypertext formats.

Evaluation

The major strengths of the Clearinghouse stem from a firm embrace of the value added approach and a distributed model for online publishing. By encouraging authors all over the world, many of whom are subject specialists, to develop value added guides by identifying, selecting, organizing, describing, and evaluating Internet information resources, the Clearinghouse takes advantage of the capabilities for communication and collaboration via the Internet and taps the skills, knowledge, and energy of willing individuals on a global scale. Some of the top guides serve as the single best source of Internet based information on a particular subject. If you're planning a comprehensive search on a specific topic, the Clearinghouse is a great place to start. If a guide on that topic exists, much of your work may already be done.

The major weaknesses of the Clearinghouse also arise from the value added approach and the distributed model. Coverage of many topics is sparse or non-existent due to a limited number of people who have found the time or interest to develop a guide on a particular subject. Also, the quality varies significantly from guide to guide. Some guides are relatively comprehensive, well organized, and current. Others are not.

Sample Search

Objective: Charles would like to find some of the better model railroading resources on the Internet.

From the main menu, Charles has a choice of 12 general subject categories. Of those categories "Arts & Entertainment" looks the most promising. He selects that category which takes him to a listing of guides organized alphabetically by keyword. He selects "Railroad" and finds himself on a title page which provides information about the author and a link to the guide itself which is in hypertext format.

The main page of the guide tells him "This WWW server provides a catalog of pointers to interesting and important railroad-related information sources on the Internet. Some model-railroading information is also included." The table of contents lists commercial online services, newsletters, databases, and model railroad information. He selects "Model Railroad Information" and is rewarded with an extensive list of resources complete with descriptions. This section does not provide evaluative information and is not particularly well organized, but it does connect him with an excellent variety of interesting model railroading resources.

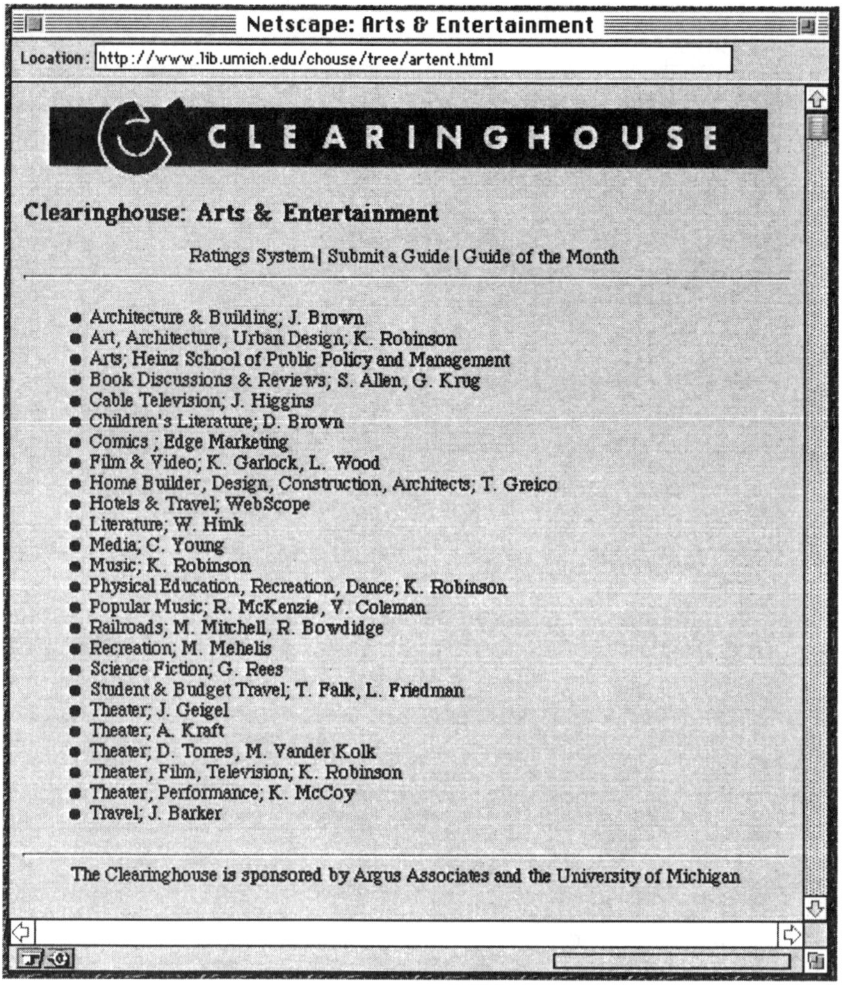

Figure 5–2   The Arts & Entertainment Category of the Clearinghouse

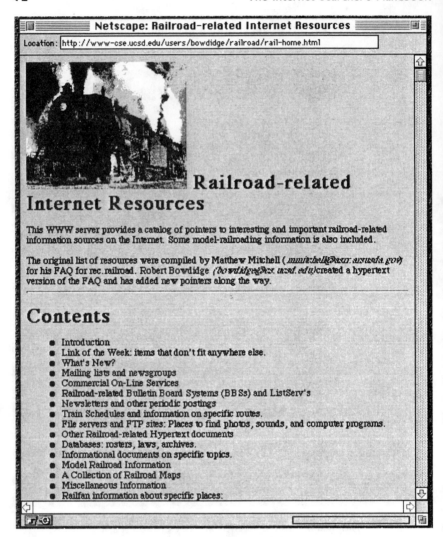

Figure 5–3   The Guide to Railroad-Related Internet Resources

INTERNET PUBLIC LIBRARY

Meta Information

URL:	http://ipl.org/
Resource Type:	World Wide Web site
Use:	finding the most useful and interesting information resources, software, and online communities on a particular topic; useful for reference and research; asking online reference questions
Navigation:	browse using traditional library metaphor, browse subject hierarchy, search using keywords, ask for help
Scope:	broad, with the following top level categories: general reference, business and economics, computers, education, entertainment, environment, government and law, health and nutrition, humanities, Internet, libraries and librarians, news and current events, science, social issues and social services
Volume:	roughly 250 resources
Searching Tips:	browse the general categories; if that fails, try the keyword searching; as a last resort, submit an online reference question
Strengths:	well organized, resources of consistent high quality, interactive reference component
Weaknesses:	limited number of topics and resources, overuse of graphics
Updates:	variable
Questions:	ipl@umich.edu
Submissions:	http://ipl.sils.umich.edu/ref/RR/recommend.html

Figure 5–4   The Internet Public Library

Description

The Internet Public Library is more than just a virtual library. Using a metaphor for a traditional library, the IPL is organized into a number of divisions including reference, youth, and librarian services. For the purposes of this book, we are concerned primarily with the reference department. The Internet Public Library expands on the value added concept by bringing online reference librarians into the picture. Questions can be submitted using online forms, e-mail, or an object oriented multiuser environment which facilitates real-time interaction between librarians and patrons. The Internet Public Library also provides a "ready reference" section which meets our standard definition of a virtual library. The ready reference section provides topical categories for browsing and a query interface for keyword searching. Pursuing the goal of fast and easy access to information, the IPL includes a limited set of high quality resources. In addition to direct links, descriptive, and evaluative information is provided for each resource.

Evaluation

The ready reference section of the Internet Public Library is an excellent tool for quickly finding a few high quality resources on a given topic. It is one of the best places to go on the Internet if you are looking for a specific answer to a factual question. A well designed organization scheme combines with the keyword searching tool to allow for fast, easy access to information. The weakness of the Internet Public Library lies in the depth of coverage on any given topic. Since the Internet Public Library only selects the best resources for each topic and only includes resources on a limited number of topics, many valuable sources of information are missed. This weakness is addressed to some extent by the availability of reference librarians who will attempt to help users with their questions. Although this model has some obvious problems, for now it appears to work quite well. A final problem with the Internet Public Library arises from the overuse of graphics. Users are forced to choose between an attractive yet very slow graphical display and a much less attractive but faster text display.

Sample Search

Objective: Paul would like to find some free stock quote services.

From the main menu of the "Ready Reference Collection," Paul can browse through the subject categories or search by keywords. First, he decides to try the query interface which allows him to perform Boolean searches and to specify author and subject category fields. Paul enters "stocks" into the general query box and is rewarded with seven hits. He browses the results, which provide the title, author, keywords, and a brief description for each resource, and he finds a couple of stock quote services. Returning to the main menu, he browses through the subject categories and selects "Business and Economics." He then browses through several sub-categories, chooses "Stocks, " and finds the same stock quote services. Both the browsing and searching capabilities provide fast and

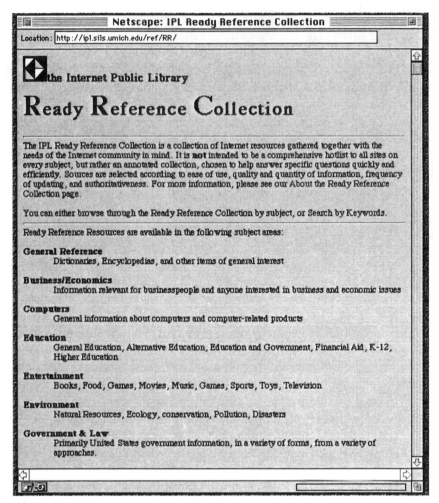

Figure 5–5   The Ready Reference Collection of the IPL

easy access to the resources. Paul decides to ask an IPL reference librarian whether any European or Japanese stock quote services are available on the Internet. He can choose whether to submit his question via e-mail or an online form. Within a few hours, an IPL librarian responds via e-mail with a couple of interesting services to try out.

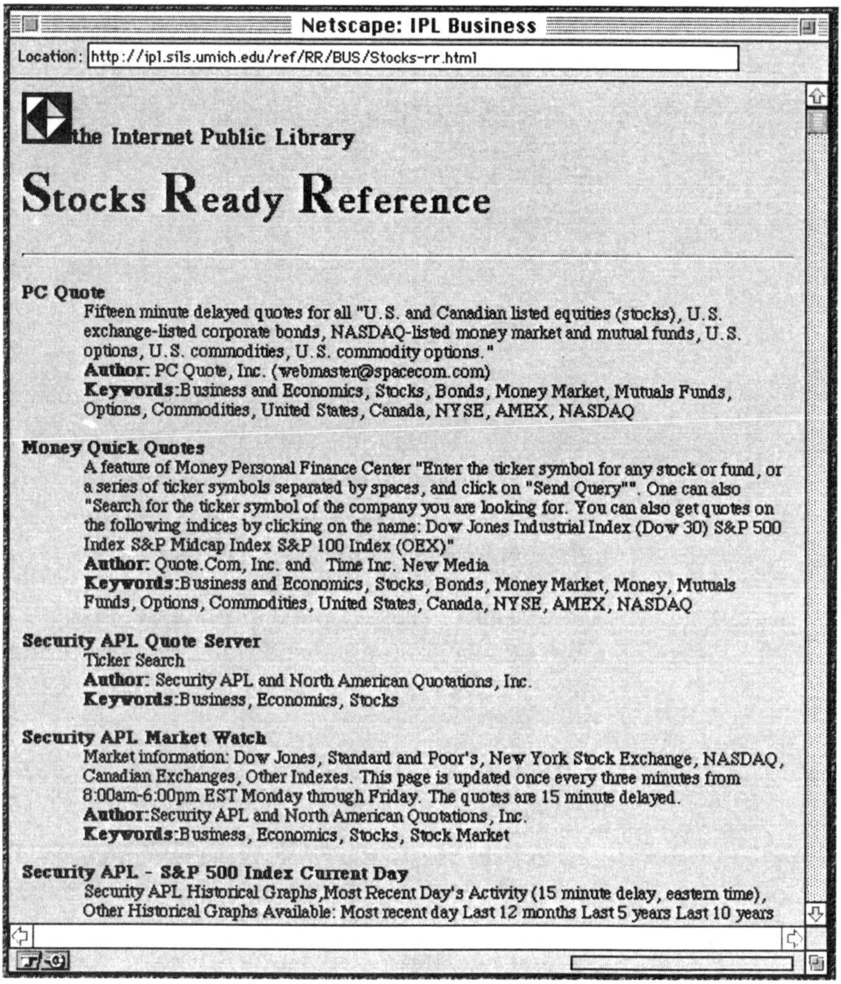

```
===================== Netscape: IPL Business =====================
Location: http://ipl.sils.umich.edu/ref/RR/BUS/Stocks-rr.html
```

◆the Internet Public Library

Stocks Ready Reference

PC Quote
Fifteen minute delayed quotes for all "U.S. and Canadian listed equities (stocks), U.S. exchange-listed corporate bonds, NASDAQ-listed money market and mutual funds, U.S. options, U.S. commodities, U.S. commodity options."
Author: PC Quote, Inc. (webmaster@spacecom.com)
Keywords: Business and Economics, Stocks, Bonds, Money Market, Mutuals Funds, Options, Commodities, United States, Canada, NYSE, AMEX, NASDAQ

Money Quick Quotes
A feature of Money Personal Finance Center "Enter the ticker symbol for any stock or fund, or a series of ticker symbols separated by spaces, and click on "Send Query"". One can also "Search for the ticker symbol of the company you are looking for. You can also get quotes on the following indices by clicking on the name: Dow Jones Industrial Index (Dow 30) S&P 500 Index S&P Midcap Index S&P 100 Index (OEX)"
Author: Quote.Com, Inc. and Time Inc. New Media
Keywords: Business and Economics, Stocks, Bonds, Money Market, Money, Mutuals Funds, Options, Commodities, United States, Canada, NYSE, AMEX, NASDAQ

Security APL Quote Server
Ticker Search
Author: Security APL and North American Quotations, Inc.
Keywords: Business, Economics, Stocks

Security APL Market Watch
Market information: Dow Jones, Standard and Poor's, New York Stock Exchange, NASDAQ, Canadian Exchanges, Other Indexes. This page is updated once every three minutes from 8:00am-6:00pm EST Monday through Friday. The quotes are 15 minute delayed.
Author: Security APL and North American Quotations, Inc.
Keywords: Business, Economics, Stocks, Stock Market

Security APL - S&P 500 Index Current Day
Security APL Historical Graphs ,Most Recent Day's Activity (15 minute delay, eastern time), Other Historical Graphs Available: Most recent day Last 12 months Last 5 years Last 10 years

Figure 5–6   Stock Quote Services in the IPL

MAGELLAN INTERNET DIRECTORY

Meta Information

URL:	http://mckinley.mckinley.com/
Resource Type:	World Wide Web site
Use:	finding information resources and online communities; primarily useful for research but may also help with some reference queries
Navigation:	browse the subject hierarchy; search the full text of resource titles and descriptions
Scope:	broad, with the following top level categories: arts and music, business and economics, communications, computing and mathematics, education, engineering and technology, government and politics, health and medicine, humanities and social sciences, Internet, law and criminal justice, popular culture and entertainment, religion and philosophy, science, sports and recreation
Volume:	80,000 resources; 20,000 are evaluated, rated, and reviewed
Searching Tips:	take advantage of the Boolean capabilities (and, or, not); proximity, adjacency, and stemming are also possible; it can also be useful to limit by category or minimum rating
Strengths:	descriptions, evaluations, and ratings for each resource; only the most interesting resources for each category; a powerful search interface combined with a well designed subject hierarchy
Weaknesses:	not as comprehensive or up to date as many of the Internet directories
Updates:	weekly
Questions:	mckinley@mckinley.com
Submissions:	http://www.mckinley.com/Template_new.html

Figure 5–7   The Magellan Internet Directory

Description

The Magellan Internet Directory (despite its name) *is* a virtual library which provides descriptions, evaluations, and ratings for a wide variety of Web sites, Usenet newsgroups, and electronic mailing lists. The distinguishing feature of the Magellan is the evaluation scheme. Resources are evaluated using a one to four star rating system that takes into account coverage, organization, currency, and ease of access. Descriptions, intended audience, keywords, and other meta information are also provided. Users may browse through the subject hierarchy or search the full text of titles and resource descriptions and evaluations. Advanced search capabilities include Boolean logic (and, or, not), proximity and adjacency searching, and the use of wildcards for word stemming. Users may limit searches by subject category or minimum rating.

Evaluation

The Magellan is an excellent resource for finding several high-quality resources on a given topic. The topical hierarchy is well designed, the search interface is powerful yet easy to use, the search engine is fast, and the results are well presented. The integration of descriptions with an evaluation scheme makes the Magellan a very interesting and useful tool. On the down side, the Magellan is far from comprehensive, even when compared with other virtual libraries. The labor necessary to review, describe, and evaluate each resource limits the number of resources that can be covered.

Sample Search

Objective: Edith would like to find some interesting genealogy resources.

Edith begins by browsing through the subject hierarchy. She tries "Humanities and Social Sciences" first but with no luck. She then tries "Popular Culture and Entertainment" where she finds five resources listed under genealogy. The resources are listed by title with a rating noted by stars, a detailed description, a link to the full record for that resource, and a link directly to the site. The full record provides keyword, audience, description, language, producer, contact e-mail, and cost fields as well as a rating summary.

After reviewing the resources, Edith tries using the query interface. She searches on "genealogy" and sets three stars (***) as her minimum rating. She is rewarded with 12 records that match her query.

PLANET EARTH VIRTUAL LIBRARY

Meta Information

URL:	http://www.nosc.mil/planet_earth/info.html
Resource Type:	World Wide Web site
Use:	finding useful or popular Internet sites, finding information resources; reference and research
Navigation:	browse topical image map or library floor plan, search using keywords
Scope:	broad with hundreds of top level categories
Volume:	over 220 sub-categories
Searching Tips:	the comprehensive image map is the best way to quickly access information; alternatively, you might try the query interface
Strengths:	fast access to some unusual and interesting sources of information
Weaknesses:	confusing organizational schemes
Updates:	weekly
Questions:	Richard P. Bocker, bocker@nosc.mil
Submissions:	n/a

Description

The Planet Earth Virtual Library provides pointers to a large but somewhat arbitrary collection of information resources available via the World Wide Web. Three navigation tools provide access to the resources. First, a graphical image map provides direct access to all 238 categories. Some of the categories refer to topics, some to types of tools, and some to organizations responsible for the content of particular sites. Second, a floor plan divides the information into 13 rooms including one each for search engines, reference, science, education, government, and multimedia. Graphical and text based interfaces are available. Third, a search engine provides keyword access to the resources.

Evaluation

The most interesting feature of the Planet Earth Virtual Library is the comprehensive image map which provides direct access to hundreds of World Wide Web sites. The flattened organizational hierarchy provides users with a quick means of scanning the available resources. The virtual floor plan is also an interesting way of organizing information. However, the Planet Earth Virtual Library suffers from rather confusing categorization and selection of information resources. With some categories referring to topics, some to types of tools, and some to the organizations responsible for content, the image map is confusing and difficult to navigate. Also, the sources of information range from the very general to the very specific, creating further confusion. Finally, the index used for conducting queries seems to be fairly poor. Searches on fairly general keywords such as "psychology" return few if any hits. In summary, the Planet Earth Virtual Library is worth a visit, but is not currently a good tool for conducting reference or research.

Sample Search

Objective: Jasmine wants to find a picture of the English flag.

From the main page, Jasmine selects the comprehensive image map where she scans through the categories until she finds "flags" under the heading of "multimedia." This takes her directly to a listing of flag related resources, including a directory of flags of the world. Using the virtual floor plan, her first inclination is to try "World Room" one or two. After finding nothing in those areas, Jasmine returns to the virtual floor plan and selects the "Multimedia Room" where she finds the flags menu. Finally, using the query interface she searches on the keyword "flag" and is rewarded with a list of hits, one of which is the multimedia menu.

SPECIAL INTERNET CONNECTIONS (THE YANOFF LIST)

Meta Information

URL:	http://www.uwm.edu/Mirror/inet.services.html
Resource Type:	World Wide Web site
Use:	finding the most useful or interesting information resources, software, and online communities within a particular topic; reference and research
Navigation:	browse subject hierarchy
Scope:	broad, with over 40 top level categories
Volume:	over 300 unique resources
Searching Tips:	select the appropriate top level category and scan the resources; you might also try using the search capability of your World Wide Web browser to find specific resources
Strengths:	fast easy access to information, good descriptive information
Weaknesses:	sparse coverage of some topics, no searching tool
Updates:	weekly
Questions:	Scott Yanoff, yanoff@alpha2.csd.uwm.edu
Submissions:	n/a

Description

Special Internet Connections, also known as the Yanoff List, is a collection of pointers to hundreds of Internet information resources. Only the best resources for any given topic are included. Descriptive information is provided for a subset of these resources. Navigation is possible using a detailed hierarchical categorization scheme. No searching capability is provided.

Evaluation

Special Internet Connections provides fast, easy access to a substantial portion of the most interesting and useful resources on the Internet. The

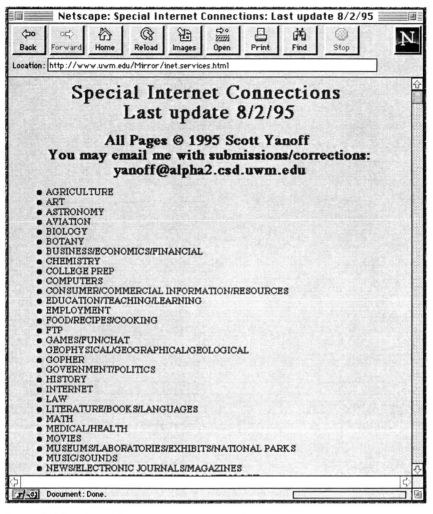

Figure 5–10   Scott Yanoff's Special Internet Connections

organizational scheme is well designed and the page layout is excellent. Special Internet Connections is an excellent tool for conducting quick reference queries and a very valuable resource when conducting more extensive research investigations.

Special Internet Connections, like all virtual libraries, suffers from sparse or non-existent coverage of some topics and a lack of currency on all topics. In addition, a keyword search tool is sorely missing. Finally, the use of all capital letters for labeling of the top level categorization scheme makes it rather difficult to skim the page quickly.

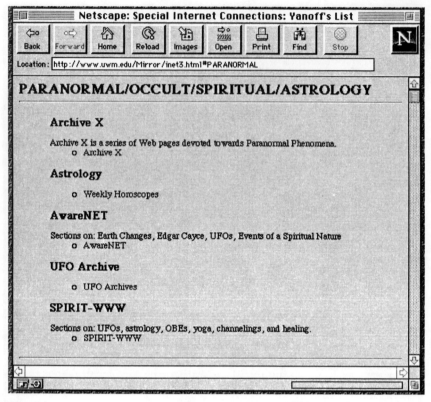

Figure 5–11   Special Internet Connections' Paranormal Category

Sample Search

Objective: Steve would like to find some information about UFO's.

From the main menu, Steve browses through the extensive list of categories and selects "PARANORMAL/OCCULT/SPIRITUAL/ASTROLOGY." From there, he browses through an alphabetical listing of resources, some with descriptions, until he finds a site entitled "UFO Archives."

WHOLE INTERNET CATALOG

Meta Information

URL:	http://www.gnn.com/gnn/wic/index.html
Resource Type:	World Wide Web site
Use:	finding the most useful and interesting information resources, software, and online communities on a particular topic; good for reference and research; if you're new to the Internet, this is a great place to get a sense of the types of resources available
Navigation:	browse subject hierarchy or view top 50 resources
Scope:	broad, with the following top level categories: arts and entertainment, business and finance, computers, daily news, education, government, health and medicine, humanities, Internet, recreation, sports and hobbies, science and technology, social sciences, travel
Volume:	roughly 20 sub-categories, each with five to ten resources
Searching Tips:	browsing the list of sub-categories is the best way to find topical information
Strengths:	well organized, resources of consistent high quality
Weaknesses:	limited number of topics covered, often rather slow
Updates:	weekly
Questions:	forum@gnn.com
Submissions:	n/a

Figure 5–12   The Whole Internet Catalog. GNN is a trademark of America Online, Inc. Copyright © 1995 by America Online, Inc. Reprinted with permission.

Description

The Whole Internet Catalog is a collection of pointers to resources in more than 150 specific subject areas, including photography, literature, and mathematics. In addition to direct links, descriptive and evaluative information is provided for each resource. The distinguishing features of the Whole Internet Catalog derive from the centralized and commercial nature of its development and management. The hierarchy has been carefully developed by staff at GNN, the sponsoring organization. Resources are selected, organized, described, and evaluated by GNN staff. GNN's decision to include only the best resources for each topic provides another major distinction from other virtual libraries. A number of relatively unobtrusive advertisements scattered throughout the navigational pages belie the commercial nature of the Whole Internet Catalog.

Evaluation

The combination of the value added approach with a successful economic model has permitted the development of a well organized virtual library which provides excellent descriptive and evaluative information for each resource. The high level of editorial control removes the need for users to sift through dozens of resources in search of accurate, current, or well organized information resources. If you're looking for a few interesting resources on a particular topic, the Whole Internet Catalog is the place to visit.

The centralized approach to information management exhibited by the Whole Internet Catalog presents a weakness as well as a strength. The team of "digital librarians" at GNN can only maintain so many subject categories and pointers to resources at once. For this reason, the variety of topics is somewhat limited. Finally, the popularity of the Whole Internet Catalog combined with the extensive use of graphics produce relatively slow access. Consider turning off your image display capabilities when visiting this site.

Sample Search

Objective: Mary would like to find a few interesting gardening resources.

From the main menu, Mary browses through the major headings until she finds "Recreation, Sports, and Hobbies." Within that topic, Mary selects the sub-category entitled "Gardening," and is rewarded with pointers to five Web sites and a Usenet newsgroup. Upon selecting the first pointer, "Bonsai," she is presented with a brief description and evaluation of the resource. At this point she can choose to visit the site or return to the list of pointers.

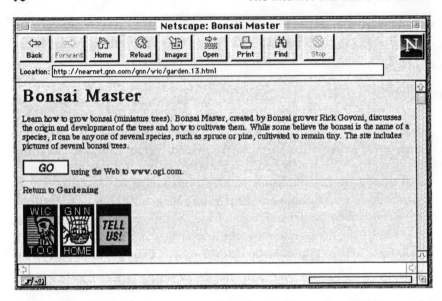

Figure 5–13   The WIC's Description of the Bonsai Master Site. GNN is a trademark of America Online, Inc. Copyright © 1995 by America Online, Inc. Reprinted with permission.

WORLD WIDE WEB VIRTUAL LIBRARY

Meta Information

URL:	http://www.w3.org/hypertext/DataSources/ bySubject/Overview.html
Resource Type:	World Wide Web site
Use:	finding information resources, software, and online communities; best for conducting research but may help with some reference queries; best for finding a variety of useful resources under a broad heading; most useful for queries that don't require current information
Navigation:	browse subject and resource type hierarchies, search full text index
Scope:	broad with over 100 top level categories
Volume:	over 100 categories; note that each category includes dozens or hundreds of resources
Searching Tips:	select a broad category and scan the section headings; you might also try keyword searching the CUI W3 Catalog (see page 130) which indexes the W3 Virtual Library and a number of other sources
Strengths:	certain topics covered extremely well
Weaknesses:	sparse coverage of some topics, variable quality from topic to topic, poor top level organizational scheme
Updates:	variable depending upon the maintainer of each subject category
Questions:	Arthur Secret, vlib@info.cern.ch
Submissions:	http://www.w3.org/hypertext/DataSources/ bySubject/Maintainers.html

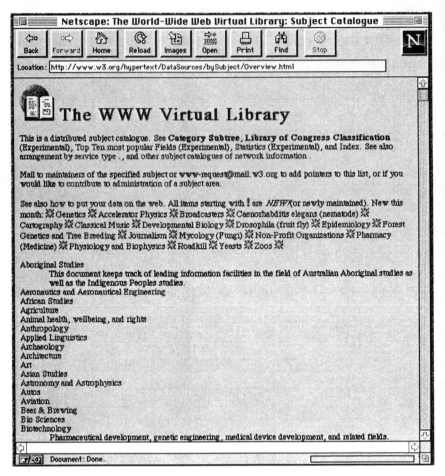

Figure 5–14   The World Wide Web Virtual Library

Description

The W3 Virtual Library is a catalog of over 100 subject specific Web sites which provide topical access to thousands of Internet information resources. Topics range from aboriginal studies, to beer and brewing, to paranormal phenomena. Most of the topical Web sites organize the resources by subject and provide descriptions of and links to those resources. Some of the sites also provide evaluative information. While a number of the categories continue to be maintained by volunteer staff at CERN, the sponsoring organization, many categories are maintained by subject experts on remote servers around the world. The W3 Virtual Library consists mostly of hypertext based information, but some other formats, such as Gopher and FTP sites, are included.

Evaluation

The major strengths of the W3 Virtual Library derive from its success at enlisting the help of volunteers who contribute their time and energy to the development and maintenance of topical categories. Although the value added approach is not explicitly encouraged, many site developers provide subject oriented organization schemes and descriptive information which makes information access much more efficient. Some of these topical Web sites in the W3 Virtual Library serve as the single best source of Internet based information on a particular subject. If you're conducting a comprehensive search on a specific topic, be sure to take a look at the W3 Virtual Library.

As with the Clearinghouse, the major weaknesses of the W3 Virtual Library are inherent in the value added, distributed, volunteer driven model. Coverage of many topics is sparse or non-existent due to a limited number of people who have found the time or interest to develop a Web site on a particular subject. In addition, the quality varies substantially from site to site. Some are relatively comprehensive, well organized, and current. Others are not. Another problem with the W3 Virtual Library stems from the top level organization scheme which consists of over 100 categories. The page layout is rather disorganized and the choice of categories somewhat haphazard.

Sample Search

Objective: Carl hopes to find some information about the history of architecture.

From the main menu, Carl has a choice of over 100 subject categories, some broad and some very specific. He also has the option to search through these categories using the W3 Catalog (see page 130). He tries a quick search on the keyword "architecture" and the search engine returns a rather long list of specific architecture related resources. Carl decides to try the browsing approach instead, returns to the main menu, and selects "Architecture." The Web site organizes architectural information into roughly 20 categories, one of which is "history." A query box is also provided for conducting specific searches. Carl selects "history" and is rewarded with a list of 22 pointers to Web sites on the topic of architectural history.

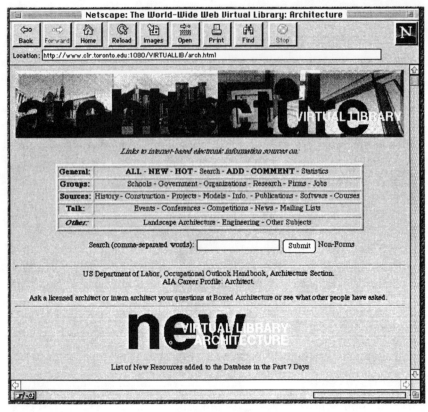

Figure 5–15   The Architecture Section of the World Wide Web Virtual Library

Chapter Six

Internet Directories

Contents

AN OVERVIEW OF INTERNET DIRECTORIES

Internet directories or "collections of resources maintained by the global Internet community" are currently the most comprehensive, easy to use tools for finding Internet information. Consequently, they are the most popular. Yahoo, the best known tool in the category, has practically become a household name, albeit a strange one. Internet directories combine the features and capabilities of both virtual libraries and Internet search tools, balancing central control with distributed independence, and melding the efforts of human and machine.

Directories provide an organizational scheme to facilitate browsing. Topical, geographical, and alphabetical naming schemes are most common. The top levels of the organizational hierarchy are created by the managers of the directory. The creation of lower level categories is often left to the Internet community. Any person or business can "publish" their information in these directories. For each resource, directories typically include only a title, although brief descriptive and evaluative information may also be presented. Many of the resource entries are provided by individuals or organizations who want to make sure that people will find their information. These information providers typically have control over the content of their descriptive and evaluative information and the location of their resource within the hierarchy, as long as they conform to a set of guidelines. Other resource entries are collected by automated search engines and intelligent agents that roam the Internet looking for new information resources. Pre-assigned keywords are used in the retrieval and organization of these resources. Depending upon the directory, varying levels of editorial control are applied to resources submitted for inclusion by human users or electronic agents.

In addition to the organizational hierarchy, a query interface is typically provided to facilitate searching. The searching capabilities vary widely from directory to directory and may allow keyword, field specific, and/or full text searching.

Strengths

With several million potential contributors (some human and some machine), the strength of Internet directories clearly lies in their ability to be relatively comprehensive and up to date. The information in directories is made intellectually accessible through a varying combination of editorial control, placement within the organizational hierarchy, and the application of search capabilities. With a powerful search engine and flexible query interface, finding useful information resources can be fast and easy. At present, Internet directories are the premiere tools for finding Internet information resources.

Weaknesses

The weakness of Internet directories lies in the lack of editorial control over content and organization. The sheer volume of resources submitted for inclusion makes it virtually impossible for the directory managers to review each resource for quality, currency, and appropriateness within a given organizational category. They certainly don't have time to describe and evaluate each resource. These editorial duties are passed on to users (who may or may not describe their resource properly) or to automated processes. For this reason, a search in a directory may return a number of false drops and several low quality or out of date resources. The burden for sifting through these pointers is placed on the user.

Searching Tips

Internet directories are useful for both reference and research. When looking for a few useful resources on a given topic, the search capabilities of these directories is your best bet for fast, easy access. Try a specific term or keyword first and if that doesn't work, broaden your search. When conducting a more comprehensive research investigation, a combination of searching and browsing will serve you best.

Considerations for the Future

Internet directories are today's tool of choice for finding Internet information resources. However, there is a very real danger that in the not so distant future these directories will collapse under their own weight. As the volume of Internet information continues to increase exponentially, it will become more and more difficult to add new resources in a timely fashion, especially if editorial control is attempted. As more and more categories are added to the organizational hierarchy, browsing will become inefficient and frustrating. As vast numbers of resources of widely varying quality are added, users will increasingly be forced to sift through hundreds or thousands of hits to find some useful information.

Over time, the managers of Internet directories will need to tweak the levels of centralized versus decentralized editorial control and human versus automated information selection, description, evaluation, and organization. This tweaking will affect the balance between comprehensiveness, timeliness, and ease of use. Like everything else in this environment, Internet directories will need to change to keep up with the increasing demands of users and the rapidly evolving Internet.

A DEVELOPER'S PERSPECTIVE

by Stephanie Walker
Galaxy Information Specialist, TradeWave Corporation

It is easy to get lost on the Internet. One minute you may be visiting a place where you can peruse a collection of photographs, then, at the click of your mouse, you suddenly could be reading an article about dental implants. There is no doubt about the wealth of information that is available to everyone who uses the Internet. What is doubtful is how you will ever find exactly what you are looking for.

Fortunately, there is help. Galaxy is an Internet directory that is being developed to assist Internet users in locating the kind of information they desire. Galaxy was introduced as a non-profit venture in January of 1994. It was one of the first directory services to join the WWW's hypertext capabilities with WAIS searching and has since become one of the top three Internet directory services in the world. In April of 1995, Galaxy became a commercial service as part of TradeWave Corporation (formerly EINet).

Organizations are allowed to purchase advertising space on Galaxy. However, there is no cost to anyone who requests that their site be listed in Galaxy and no cost to users. In addition to offering this free service, it is also important to us that the advertising on Galaxy does not interfere with serious researchers. Every Galaxy user who has a question about either using the directory or being listed there is encouraged to contact us. We are also always open to suggestions for improving our service.

Galaxy is a general Internet directory. The types of sites it contains can be divided into three basic categories: academic, commercial, and social. These categories are further broken down into specific areas such as Poetry, Real Estate, and World Communities. Galaxy is the only major directory to describe its entries by the type of information each contains. A few of the different types are:

Articles:	short, stand-alone text, usually about a single subject.
Events:	description and information pertaining to an event.
Directories:	lists of links to other sites, which usually share a common theme.
Academic Organizations:	information about a school, college, or university.
Commercial Organizations:	information about a corporation or company
Product/Service Descriptions:	description of specific products and/or services.

Galaxy is searchable in two ways. First, users may simply browse through over 1,100 subject headings which are hierarchically arranged from broad to specific. This works for users who are not exactly sure of what they are seeking. The second way to search Galaxy is by formulating search keywords and using the Boolean-based search engine. Galaxy allows users to search different parameters of the database. For example, users may search only the titles of sites within Galaxy, they may search the full text of all the sites indexed in Galaxy, or they may search all of the links that are within those sites. Galaxy also allows users to search Gopher menus and telnet sites as well as the Galaxy pages themselves. All of these different methods of searching allow individuals to customize their search strategies to exactly suit their needs.

We are also in the process of creating annotations for most of the sites listed in Galaxy that will help the user choose which links best meet his or her needs. The topical arrangement of Galaxy is currently undergoing a massive restructuring that includes the development of more subject headings and cross references. Galaxy will continue to evolve as it gathers more sites which contain new types of information.

The process of cataloging or indexing the Internet is a part of the new frontier for information professionals. As such, it has all of the excitement and the aggravation of formulating new standards. Since there is no controlled vocabulary, the task of organizing sites under subject headings is quite challenging and a bit overwhelming. Adding to this is the huge number of sites that are being created daily on the Web. The volume of requests to be added to Galaxy has almost tripled in the past two months. Since each request is handled individually by a Galaxy editor who assigns it to the proper topic, the issues involved in indexing the Internet are confronted daily. Without universal guidelines the process of classifying sites will remain extremely subjective for all directories.

Unfortunately, there are not many professional librarians involved in the development of most commercial directories. Therefore, the criteria for classifying Internet sites are slow to be developed. At Galaxy, we hope to influence the development of a set of standards for indexing that can be applied to information on the global Internet where controlled vocabulary does not and most likely will never exist.

One of the classic indexing problems we have had to overcome is that many sites cannot easily be classified under just one or two subject headings. For example, a commercial site may sell clothing, furniture, and sporting goods. All of these are consumer goods, but in order to accurately index this site, it must be listed at least three times, which takes personnel time and company disk space. Hence, Galaxy's extensive use of cross-references. We want to provide as much access as possible without being too redundant and without using an excessive amount of our resources. Therefore, an entry may be listed up to two or three times, but if it needs more subject headings, the cross-references come into play.

Another area of challenge is that many individuals are creating their own "home pages." These sites are full of sundry information from what the creator had for dinner last night to excellent lists of links to sources on specific topics such as cancer research. It can be hard to decide to list such sites under "Cancer" when half of the page is also dedicated to the creator's personal life, which may or may not have anything to do with cancer.

There is no easy way to index personal home pages. Until a "white pages" type of system is developed for the Internet, personal home pages will most likely be organized alphabetically or geographically. The problem with both of these types of organization is that some people do not use their real names or even a name at all and others do not reveal where they are geographically located.

Like many information sources, Galaxy has also had to develop policies for dealing with the question of listing sites that contain pornography, pro-drug information, and other controversial material. Since Galaxy is a private commercial entity, we are able to decide what kinds of sites we will and will not include in Galaxy. This type of selection is done by most Internet directories. Some other directories will only include sites that they deem to have "valuable" information. Other directories only list sites that have paid to be listed there. Which of the directories is most useful will be determined by the type of information being sought by the individual consumer.

It is important to keep in mind that not all sites are listed in any one Internet directory. Some are more comprehensive than others. Some specialize in certain areas. A combination of learning good search strategies and finding the right directory will enable users to get the most out of Internet directories. As more and more people gain access to the Internet, directories will continue to evolve and become more useful for weeding through the incredible amount of information being created.

Perhaps someday there will be virtual reality directories modelled after the physical library building. Users will stroll through the doors of the directory and be able to browse the shelves which are filled with books that represent links to Internet sites around the world. Opening a book will result in the user being "transported" to another locale within the Internet. Because Internet directories are growing and changing so rapidly, there is really no telling what marvels the future holds.

BIZWEB

Meta Information

URL:	http://www.bizweb.com/
Resource Type:	World Wide Web site
Use:	finding information about companies, products, and services; primarily a reference tool
Navigation:	browse by type of company, product, or service
Scope:	company and product information
Volume:	over 700 companies
Searching Tips:	select the appropriate top level category and then use the built-in keyword searching capability of your Web browser to find the company or product you're looking for
Strengths:	descriptive information is provided for many of the companies
Weaknesses:	far fewer companies listed than some of the other directories of commercial organizations; no searching capability; too many top level categories
Updates:	weekly
Questions:	webmaster@bizweb.com
Submissions:	http://www.bizweb.com/InfoForm/infoform.html

Description

BizWeb collocates (locates together) pointers to the World Wide Web sites of over 700 companies. Users may browse by type of company, product or service. The organizational hierarchy is relatively flat, with over 50 top level categories and no sub-categories. No searching capability is available. Brief descriptions are provided for many of the companies.

Figure 6–1   BizWeb

Evaluation

BizWeb's single line descriptions makes it fairly easy to skim through the listings of companies to find what you're looking for. The avoidance of large graphics makes BizWeb fairly responsive in terms of speed.

On the down side, BizWeb is far from comprehensive. Open Market has more than ten times the number of companies listed. Also, BizWeb's organizational hierarchy is not very well developed. With 50 top level categories and no sub-categories, it's simply too flat. The presentation of those top level categories in Usenet fashion (e.g. computer.hardware.pc) is aesthetically unappealing and somewhat difficult to read. Overall, BizWeb has a long way to go before it can compete with the Open Markets of the world.

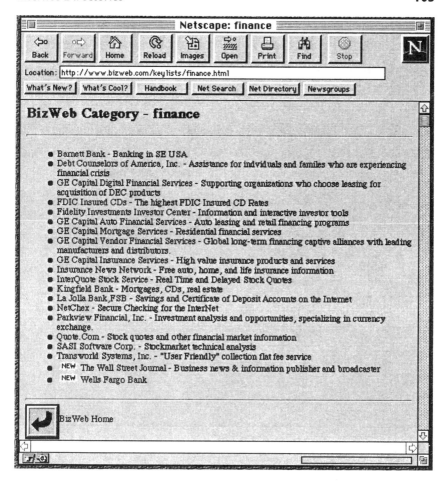

Figure 6–2   The Finance Category of BizWeb

Sample Search

Objective: Craig wants to find Fidelity Investments' information center.

From the main menu, Craig selects "finance." He skims the listings in BizWeb's finance category, until he finds "Fidelity Investments Investor Center" which is described as providing "information and interactive investor tools." This link takes Craig directly to the Investor Center.

OPEN MARKET'S COMMERCIAL SITES INDEX

Meta Information

URL:.	http://www.directory.net/
Resource Type:	World Wide Web site
Use:	finding information about companies, products, and services; primarily a reference tool
Navigation:	browse alphabetical listings and what's new list; search title, URL, and keyword fields
Scope:	Web sites or electronic storefronts for commercial organizations
Volume:	over 9,000 companies listed
Strengths:	most comprehensive and well organized directory of commercial sites
Weaknesses:	lack of subject oriented browsing capability
Updates:	daily
Questions:	editors@directory.net
Submissions:	http://www.directory.net/dir/submit.cgi

Description

Open Market's index is a directory of commercial sites on the Internet. Users can browse the alphabetical listing of over 8,000 companies or the "what's new" listing which lists companies with new Web sites and is updated daily. The entry for each company includes the name of the organization, a direct link to that company's Web site, and a list of keywords. A brief description of the company is optional. All information is provided by the companies themselves. Additionally, listings of companies providing Web space are also available for those users seeking help in establishing an Internet site for their organization. The query interface provides simple Boolean or single string searching of the title, URL, and keyword fields.

Evaluation

Open Market's index is the most comprehensive, up to date, well organized directory of commercial services on the Internet. The obvious in-

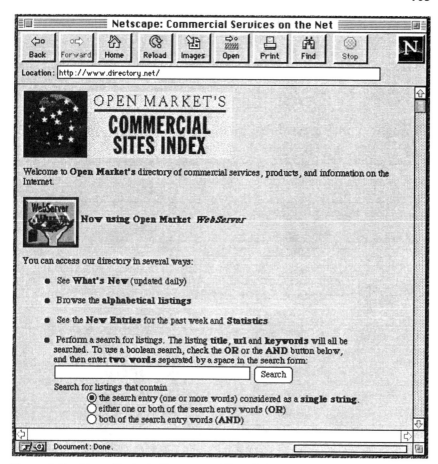

Figure 6–3   Open Market's Commercial Sites Index

centive for companies to make their information available ensures that a substantial portion of companies with Web sites list themselves in Open Market's index and provide keywords to facilitate access via the query interface. The query interface, which is easy to use but relatively flexible, is certainly the preferred means of access. Whether you're looking for a particular company or type of company, the title and keyword fields usually provide enough information to find what you need.

The alphabetical index, on the other hand, is rather cumbersome to use. With over 700 companies listed under the "A" heading, it's rather time consuming to scroll through these listings. The absence of a topical hierarchy is quite noticeable. A listing of organizations by type of product or service would be very useful.

Overall, Open Market is the best place to look for information about companies, products, or services on the Internet.

Sample Search

Objective: Gabby wants to find information about Bantam Doubleday Dell, a publishing company.

Using the alphabetical directory, Gabby selects "B," and then skims through the listings until she finds an entry for Bantam Doubleday Dell which includes a brief description and a link to the BDD Web site. Using the query interface, Gabby searches on the keyword "bantam" which brings up the BDD Web site. Entering keywords such as "book" or "magazine" or "publishing" also work.

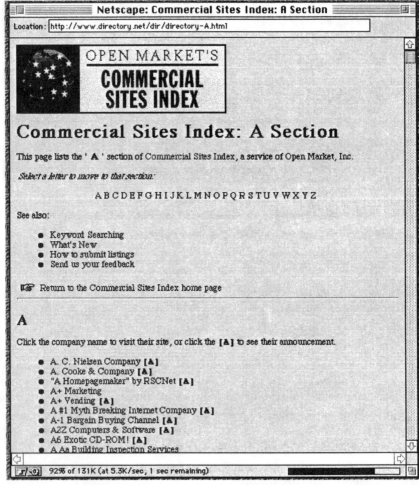

Figure 6–4   Alphabetical Index to Open Market's Directory

TRADEWAVE GALAXY

Meta Information

URL: http://www.einet.net/galaxy.html

Resource Type: World Wide Web site

Use: finding information, software, and communities of people; useful for both reference and research

Navigation: browse subject hierarchy; search category headings, resource titles, URLs, and full text

Scope: broad, with the following top level categories: arts and humanities, business and commerce, community, engineering and technology, government, law, leisure and recreation, medicine, reference and interdisciplinary information, science, social sciences

Volume: over 10,000 unique resources

Searching Tips: the extensive list of categories and sub-categories is a good place to start; on the other hand, the query interface is quite flexible and easy to use, once you understand the field definitions (which can be displayed by selecting any of the hyperlinked field titles)

Strengths: powerful search capabilities, well developed organizational scheme, nice page layout

Weaknesses: no descriptive or evaluative information, varying quality and depth of coverage from topic to topic

Updates: daily

Questions: galaxy@einet.net

Submissions: http://www.einet.net/cgi-bin/annotate?Other

Description

TradeWave Galaxy is a subject-oriented directory of Internet information resources. Users can browse using the extensive subject hierarchy or search using the query interface. The query interface allows users to perform Boolean queries on the Galaxy navigational pages, the resource titles, the full text of referenced resources, and the hypertextual links in the

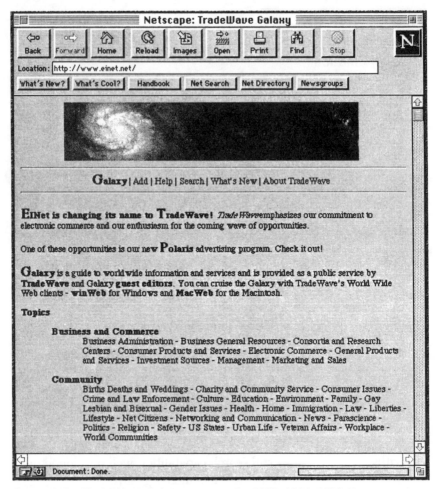

Figure 6–5   TradeWave Galaxy is copyright 1993, 1994, 1995 Enterprise Integration Network Corporation (ElNet). All rights reserved. ElNet is a trademark of ElNet, Inc.

referenced resources. Additionally, the interface permits searching of the titles of Gopher menus from Gopher Jewels and the Hytelnet database of Telnet sites.

Evaluation

The advanced query interface is certainly the most interesting feature of Galaxy. The ability to search on the indices of navigational pages, resource titles, full text, or hypertext provides the experienced searcher with substantial flexibility and power. By experimenting with the interface, precision and recall can be manipulated to suit one's purposes. The capability of searching Gopher and Telnet indices provides additional value. The subject hierarchy is well thought out but perhaps a little over developed. Some categories have only a few resources listed. The page layout of the navigational pages is clean. It appears that the Galaxy editors exercise more control over content and organization than is seen in Yahoo.

On the down side, Galaxy does not appear to be quite as comprehensive or up to date as Yahoo. Some of the pointers to resources are defunct and many new resources on the Web cannot be found in the Galaxy. Additionally, the complete absence of descriptive and evaluative information makes it difficult for users to make judgments about which resources to explore.

Overall, the Galaxy is a nicely designed navigational tool that should certainly be examined during any comprehensive research investigation and can also be quite useful for conducting reference.

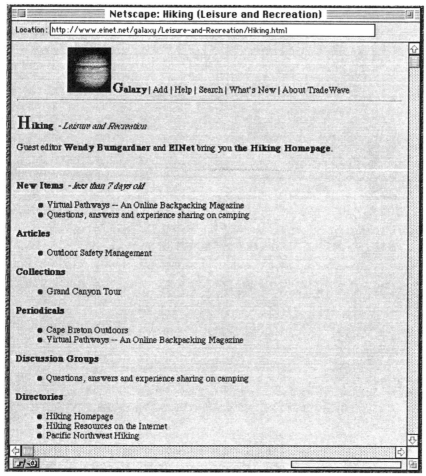

Figure 6–6   The "Hiking" Section of Galaxy

Sample Search

Objective: Lara wants to find some information about hiking.

Using the subject hierarchy, Lara finds a link to "hiking" resources listed under "leisure and recreation." The hiking menu presents her with several categories which include articles, periodicals, directories, and nonprofit organizations. There are only a couple of pointers for each category.

Using the query interface, Lara first tries searching the Galaxy navigational pages using "hiking" as her keyword. She's rewarded with a list of seven hits, ranked in order of "relevance." At the top of the list is "hiking (leisure and recreation)," the sub-category she found using the subject hierarchy. Using each of the different indices in turn, Lara gets different results. To perform a comprehensive search, it's important to try all of the indices and the subject hierarchy.

Figure 6–7   Galaxy's Query Interface

WORLD WIDE YELLOW PAGES

Meta Information

URL:	http://www.yellow.com/
Resource Type:	World Wide Web site
Use:	finding information about businesses including product, service, and contact information; finding companies' Web sites
Navigation:	browse or search by topical headings, company names, and geographical locations
Scope:	directory of World Wide Web sites or electronic storefronts for businesses
Volume:	over 26,000 entries (some companies have multiple entries)
Strengths:	multiple organizational schemes; ability to browse or search
Weaknesses:	confusing and somewhat inflexible query interface; unmanageable organizational hierarchies; response time can be very slow
Updates:	monthly
Questions:	info@yellow.com
Submissions:	http://www.yellow.com/cgi-bin/online

Description

The World Wide Yellow Pages serves as a directory and database of commercial organizations. Users can browse by headings, company names, or geographical locations. Field specific searches can be conducted using these same categories. For each organization, contact information and a brief description is provided. Information for each company is provided by users who may select whether to use an existing heading or create a new one.

Evaluation

With over 26,000 listings, the World Wide Yellow Pages is one of the more comprehensive Internet-based directories of companies. The use

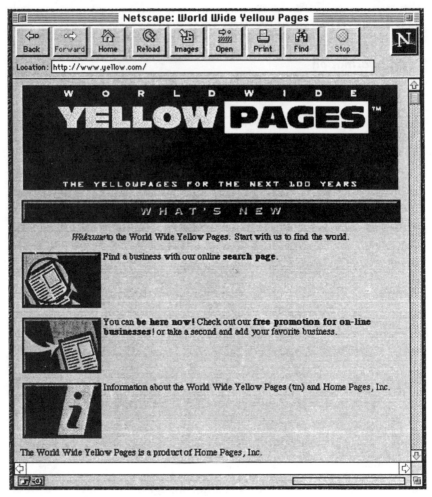

Figure 6–8   The World Wide Yellow Pages

of multiple organizational schemes and the integration of a fielded search capability promises to provide substantial flexibility in conducting a directory search. However, actual use of the World Wide Yellow Pages uncovers a number of problems with the browsing and searching capabilities. Providing users with the ability to create their own headings has led to a proliferation of headings that has rendered the "browse by headings" feature virtually useless. The "browse by location" feature suffers from similar problems. The "browse by name" feature works, but it often takes a long time for the alphabetically organized pages to load. The search functions also work, but place too much burden on the user. Wild cards must be spelled out and the search engine is unforgiving of any user mistakes. Overall, the World Wide Yellow Pages are a potentially useful but often frustrating resource for finding information about companies.

Sample Search

Objective: Betsy wants to find an online bookstore.

Using the "browse by headings" feature, Betsy selects the letter "b" and then skims through the long listing of headings. She finds one heading for technical bookstores, one for retail bookstores and one just for bookstores. Within each category Betsy finds a number of online bookstores

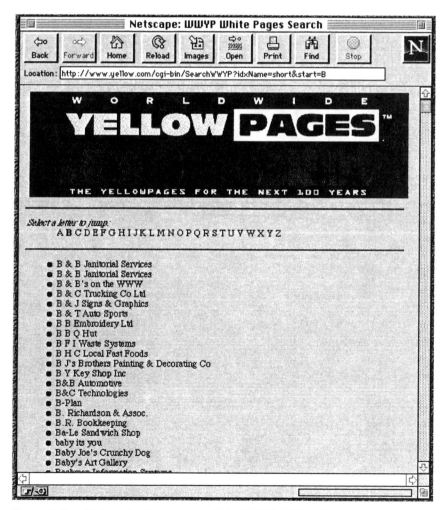

Figure 6–9   Alphabetical Index to the World Wide Yellow Pages

with contact information and direct links to their World Wide Web sites. Using the query feature, she tries a search on the word "bookstore" in the "headings" category which returns a message telling her that no such heading exists and a list of suggested headings which include "bookstores." A search on the plural word returns some useful online bookstores. This search does not return the items listed under technical or retail bookstores.

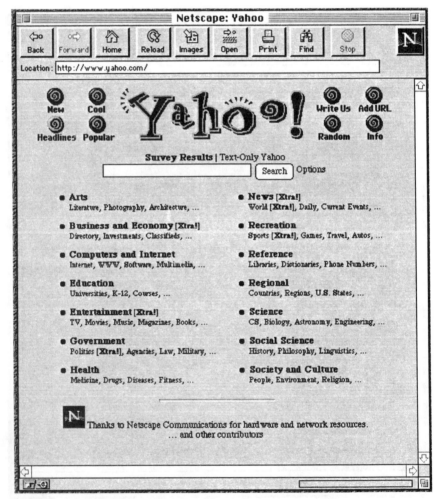

Figure 6–10   Yahoo: the most comprehensive of the Internet directories

YAHOO

Meta Information

URL:	http://www.yahoo.com/
Resource Type:	World Wide Web site
Use:	finding information, software, and people; very useful for both reference and research
Navigation:	browse subject hierarchy and lists of what's new, what's cool, what's popular, browse random links, keyword search
Scope:	broad, with the following top level categories: art, business, computers, economy, education, entertainment, environment and nature, events, government, health, humanities, law, news, politics, reference, regional information, science, social science, society and culture
Volume:	over 60,000 unique resources
Searching Tips:	given the large number of categories and resources, it's usually best to start with the query interface; if your first search returns too many hits, try a more specific combination of keywords, or try restricting your search to just the title field
Strengths:	most comprehensive, up to date Internet information retrieval resource available; fast powerful search capability
Weaknesses:	lack of editorial control over content and organization; low precision
Updates:	daily
Questions:	David Filo, filo@yahoo.com and Jerry Yang, jerry@yahoo.com
Submissions:	http://www.yahoo.com/bin/add

Description

Yahoo is the most comprehensive and up to date of the hierarchical subject-oriented directories of pointers to World Wide Web resources. Descriptive and evaluative information is provided for some of the resources. The links and information about the referenced resources are gathered in two ways. First, users may submit their own URLs and meta information. Second, automated search robots roam the Internet looking for new resources to add to Yahoo. In addition to browsing the subject hierarchy, users can view a list of what's new, what's cool, what's popular, or even a list of random links. The search interface permits users to perform Boolean queries on the title, URL, and comments fields. Case sensitive matching and substring searching are also possible. Limits can be placed on the number of hits to display.

Evaluation

As one of the most popular, comprehensive, and up to date information retrieval sites on the Internet, Yahoo's strengths are clear. Yahoo has an immense database of over 50,000 pointers to resources. Links are added on a daily basis. The subject-oriented hierarchy provides intellectual access to the resources, and is complemented by the "what's new," "cool" and "popular" lists as well as the flexible search interface. The combination of powerful computer hardware, a high speed Internet connection, and a conscious avoidance of graphics makes Yahoo one of the fastest and most reliable services on the Internet. Whether you're conducting research or seeking a quick answer to a reference question, Yahoo is one of the best places to look.

The major weaknesses of Yahoo stem from the lack of editorial control over content and organization. Anyone can submit a site, provide a description of that site, and specify the categories in which the site should be included. With the exponentially growing volume of submissions, it is impossible for the Yahoo staff to provide more than cursory quality control. It can be difficult for users to find poorly labeled resources, particularly if they are inserted into the wrong categories. Additionally, users must sift through resources of highly variable quality in their search for useful information. As the volume of Internet information continues to grow, these information retrieval problems promise to become increasingly serious.

Sample Search

Objective: John hopes to find information about SGML, an international standard for the description of marked-up electronic text.

Using the subject hierarchy, John selects "computers" and then "languages" and finally "SGML." This takes him to a menu of 11 links to SGML related resources. Brief descriptions are provided for a few of the resources. Using the query capability, John searches for the keyword "SGML" in the title, URL, and comments fields and is rewarded with 28 hits. In addition to information about the SGML language, John finds links to companies that sell SGML related products and services and user groups that meet to discuss SGML. Clearly, when attempting a comprehensive search, a combination of browsing and searching is essential.

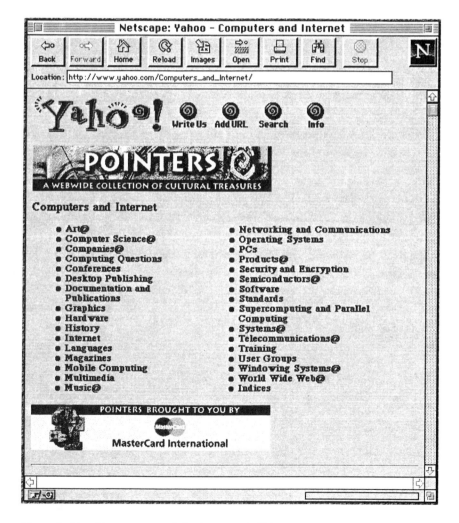

Figure 6–11   Computers and the Internet in Yahoo

Chapter Seven

Internet Search Tools

Contents

AN OVERVIEW OF INTERNET SEARCHING TOOLS

Internet searching tools constitute the richest and most varied category of resources for finding information, software, people, and communities of people on the Internet. The primary shared characteristic of these tools is the provision of keyword searching capabilities, in contrast to the emphasis placed on the browsing of hierarchical topic trees that we have seen in the virtual libraries and Internet directories. These keyword searching capabilities vary from tool to tool. Some provide only basic full text searching while others allow for the complex nesting of Boolean queries with support for proximity and adjacency searching. Tools such as Lycos make use of software robots or "spiders" that roam the World Wide Web indexing the full text of everything they find. Other tools are more specific in nature, helping users to locate and download public domain software, find contact information such as e-mail addresses and phone numbers of individuals, or locate and communicate with communities of people on a particular topic of interest.

Strengths

Internet search tools are most useful when conducting extensive research into a particular topic. When you're looking for Internet information resources, tools in this category typically allow for the most comprehensive searches. Through the use of automated software robots, powerful indexing tools, and advanced search engines, these tools are able to provide access to very large collections. The indices of some of the best tools contain the full text of several million World Wide Web documents. Flexible query interfaces provide the user with the ability to perform complex queries on these extensive document databases.

This research orientation is true, with the exception of the tools for finding people and communities of people. These tools tend to serve more of a reference function. Their strength lies in the provision of fast and easy access to white page directories of individuals and collections of online discussion groups.

Weaknesses

The primary weakness of Internet search tools arises from their dependence on automated procedures for indexing, organizing, and presenting information. The lack of editorial control over their indices leads to collections that vary widely with respect to quality, currency, and type of content. A search on the word "chemistry" may return a list of hits that includes an out of date periodic table, a very useful guide to chemistry related resources on the Internet, and a full listing of the chemistry course offerings at a university. While recall may be high, precision tends to be fairly low.

The tools for finding people and communities of people are different in this respect. These tools typically provide access to well structured databases of information. Their weaknesses often lie more in the relatively small size of these databases. They are usually far from comprehensive.

Searching Tips

Since many of these tools provide a unique way to search a unique collection of information, it's very difficult to formulate any general searching strategy. With each tool, the best path to conducting effective queries is through trial and error. Read the searching instructions, try a few searches, and learn from the results.

Considerations for the Future

The evolution of Internet search tools is blazing ahead at an astonishing rate. In a few short years, we've moved from an environment with a couple of very basic tools called Archie and Veronica to a world where just choosing the right search tool for your purposes is a challenge in itself. Some of the leading search tools of today employ intelligent software agents to scour the Internet for information, and make use of powerful query interfaces and search engines to provide users with access to these immense bodies of information. However, the rapid advances in this tool set are constantly being challenged by the exponential growth in the amount of Internet information. Within the next few years, the flexibility and power of the query interface will likely reach a plateau. The volume of Internet information will continue to grow. This will place a higher burden on the user who will need to make use of the full range of Boolean operators and proximity and adjacency capabilities in order to conduct efficient and effective searches. Another response to this problem will be increased human involvement in the identification, selection, description, evaluation, and organization of resources that make up these immense global databases of information. As the global information database continues to grow, people will place an increasingly higher value on services which facilitate fast and easy intellectual access to the information they need.

A DEVELOPER'S PERSPECTIVE

by Tim Howes
Senior Systems Research Programmer
University of Michigan's Information Technology Division
and a major developer of the QUIPU X.500 implementation

The Internet is a big place. Searching it for something in particular can be a frustrating and labor-intensive process. This is true whether one is looking for a person, a piece of software, a document, or some other resource. From a user's perspective, three main flaws in most Internet search tools cause this frustration.

1) *Difficulty in specifying and applying search criteria.* A search tool may require too much knowledge on the user's part; for example, knowledge of a restricted vocabulary or classification scheme. The scheme may make sense to its developer, but not to the user. Or, more likely, it may provide no restrictions or guidance at all, leaving the user to guess what is possible and where to begin searching. With a system like this, all information is lumped together; there is no way to separate the person *smith* from the author *smith* from the profession *smith*. This problem is at the heart of the issue, leading to the two additional problems described below.

2) *Returning too much information.* This problem leaves the user wading through lots of irrelevant information by hand, still looking for the proverbial needle in a somewhat smaller haystack. Some search tools provide some kind of relevance feedback to assist in this pro-

cess, but many do not. Such problems make automated search tool development difficult, as there is no user present to filter out the extraneous information.

3) *Returning too little information.* If the one piece of information the user wants is not returned, the search is a failure. Such failures can occur because of poorly specified search criteria, poorly cataloged data, or other reasons. Experienced users may retry the search, broadening the search criteria. Other users may take the negative result at face value and assume that the target of the search does not exist or is not available.

In many cases, the root cause of these problems is a lack of structure and organization on the information being searched.

Enter X.500, the Open Systems Interconnection directory service, based on a highly-structured information model. The X.500 model is based on entries, which are composed of attributes. An entry might represent a person, a document, or some other net or real-world resource. Each attribute has a type (e.g., commonName, or author) and one or more values (e.g., "Lou Rosenfeld"). It also has a syntax, which controls what kind of values the attribute can have and how those values behave during certain operations. For example, the *caseIgnoreString* attribute syntax allows string values which are not sensitive to case during a search or compare operation. X.500 entries are arranged in a hierarchy, allowing information, searches, authority, and administration to be distributed easily. The figure below shows an example X.500 entry for a document resource.

X.500 requires information to be strictly categorized, making specific searches easy.

title =	The Internet Searcher's Handbook
author =	Peter Morville
author =	Louis Rosenfeld
author =	Joseph Janes
publisher =	Neal-Schuman
subject =	A step-by-step guide to finding information, people, and software on the Internet.
isbn number =	1-55570-236-8
location =	ftp://host.name/path/name
keyword =	Internet
keyword=	searching
keyword=	information retrieval

The X.500 search operation provides a powerful and flexible mechanism for locating and retrieving information from the directory. A user can search various portions of the directory tree using arbitrarily complex attribute-based search criteria. X.500 supports searches for attribute equality, approximate equality, substring equality, range queries, and Boolean combinations of simpler criteria. For each entry matched, various attributes and values can be returned. Unlike many other directory systems, X.500 also provides operations for adding, deleting, and updating information in the directory.

It is important to understand that X.500 defines a protocol and corresponding information and operation models. It does not specify an implementation. This means that X.500 clients and servers may come in all shapes and sizes, with greatly varying objectives and capabilities, though they all speak the same protocols. Right now, most X.500 systems are targeted at white pages information collection and retrieval, though some sites are beginning to use their directories for more general information resources.

X.500 tools come in a variety of forms, from maX.500, waX.500 and xax500, to Macintosh, MS Windows, and X Windows based graphical user interface search tools that are highly configurable and can be used to search for all types of information, to go500gw, a Gopher-to-X.500 gateway that makes the X.500 directory information tree appear to Gopher clients as a hierarchy of menus and text documents which can be browsed and searched. Web500gw is one of several gateways that provide a similar view of X.500 from the World Wide Web via HTTP. Because X.500 defines a protocol and not an implementation, the information it contains can be presented very differently for different applications.

The X.500 directory framework allows users to make very focused and specific queries. For example, a user could search for all documents about the Internet with an author of Peter Morville; or, all Web browser software for the Macintosh updated in the last two months; or, all people named Babs Jensen in the city of Ann Arbor, Michigan. Clearly, being able to specify such queries and have them carried out accurately and efficiently provides the key to searching satisfaction on the Internet.

But what is the down side of structured information searching? Why has it not taken the Internet by storm? The answer lies in the increased effort necessary to create and gather the information that populates the directory. Each resource needs to be cataloged, attributes and values defined, etc. This is no small task given the amount of information the Internet contains. The job can be error-prone and is not easily automated. When data collection can be automated, or at least made easy and well-integrated with the Internet "publishing" process, systems like X.500 will become more widespread. Until then, X.500 faces a chicken-and-egg problem, one which it is solving so far only in the white pages information area, where it has achieved a certain critical mass of information.

Another shortcoming of X.500 in particular is its hierarchical namespace. While familiar to users and convenient for partitioning and distributing information, it can create searching inefficiencies. For example, the typical namespace is partitioned based on geographical and organizational boundaries, but the scope of a user's query may not be similarly constrainable. Either the search is constrained artificially, risking the loss of potentially valuable information, or a very broad search is conducted, wasting resources. This can be a problem.

Also hampering X.500's deployment is its general heavyweight, hard-to-run reputation. This shortcoming, along with the others, is being addressed by the Lightweight Directory Access Protocol (LDAP), currently used as a front-end to the X.500 directory. Work is underway to make LDAP into a service of its own, offering the advantages of X.500 and structured information without the high costs and sometimes draconian restrictions of X.500. This work has the potential to bring a much more capable search service to the Internet, one that serves the needs of both users and administrators, imposing some much-needed order on the chaos of the Net.

SEARCH FOR INFORMATION

ALIWEB

Meta Information

URL:	http://web.nexor.co.uk/public/aliweb/aliweb.html
Resource Type:	World Wide Web site
Use:	finding Internet information resources and services, software, and on-line communities; useful as both a research and reference tool
Navigation:	search a structured database which consists of titles, descriptions, keywords, and URLs for each resource
Scope:	very broad; users may add resources as they see fit
Volume:	6,922 resources indexed
Searching Tips:	begin with a relatively broad search, using the default values; if you don't get any hits, add URLs to the list of fields to be searched, and try a few additional keywords; if you get too many hits, try a more specific keyword and restrict the search to the title field with whole word matches only
Strengths:	a flexible and intuitive query interface combined with a record structure with title, description, keyword, and URL fields makes searching easy; the query results interface is also excellent; several mirrored sites assure fast performance
Weaknesses:	a relatively small database, when compared with other popular search tools
Updates:	daily
Questions:	Martijn Koster, m.koster@nexor.co.uk
Submissions:	http://web.nexor.co.uk/public/aliweb/doc/registering.html

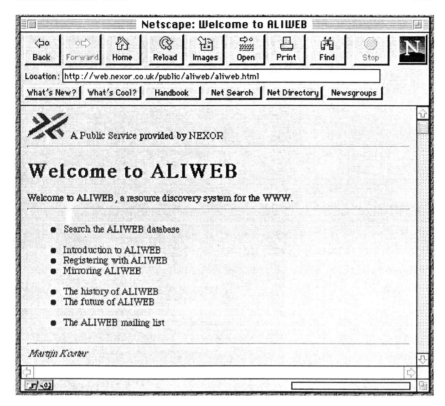

Figure 7–1   ALIWEB

Description

ALIWEB is a resource discovery system for the World Wide Web with a unique method of indexing. People who would like to have their resources indexed by ALIWEB must describe their information resource in a file, formatted in accordance with the ALIWEB specifications, on their local server. The information is divided into several fields including title, description, keyword, URL, and resource type. ALIWEB regularly retrieves and indexes these files. People may then search the ALIWEB index through a Web based query interface that allows users to restrict searches to one or more of these fields. Users may also configure the query results to display any combination of the description, keyword, URL, or other fields.

Evaluation

By enabling information providers to input and update their own records, while forcing them to conform to a structured record format, ALIWEB has developed a powerful, up to date database of Internet information resources. This database combines with the excellent query interface to make ALIWEB one of the most powerful, flexible, and easy to use search tools on the Internet. On the down side, the requirements imposed on information providers have resulted in a relatively small database.

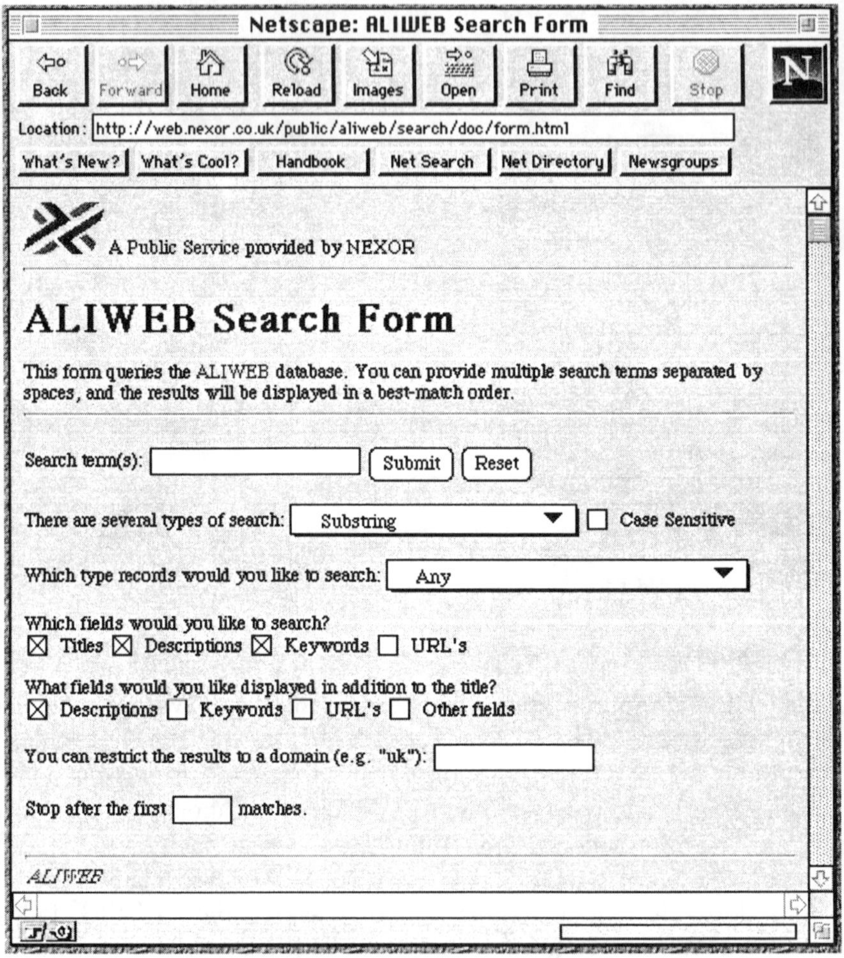

Figure 7–2   The ALIWEB Search Form

Sample Search

Objective: Beth is looking for an on-line weather service that can
                     give her a local forecast.

From the ALIWEB search form, Beth types "weather" into the query
box and selects the "submit" button. Within a few seconds the search
results page appears with titles that also serve as hyperlinks to the resources themselves and brief descriptions of each resource. Rather than
browse through the few dozen resources, Beth returns to the search form
to narrow her search. She restricts the search to the title field with whole
word expressions only and submits the new query. She is rewarded with a
list of seven hits, one of which is the Weather Gateway, a service that
provides up to date weather forecasts for major cities in the USA.

CUI W3 CATALOG

Meta Information

URL:	http://cuiwww.unige.ch/cgi-bin/w3catalog
Resource Type:	World Wide Web site
Use:	finding information resources and services, software, and on-line communities; useful as both a research and reference tool; search the full text of several popular Internet virtual libraries and directories
Navigation:	search the full text of several virtual libraries and directories using keywords; Perl regular expressions may be used (for more about regular expressions, see Appendix II)
Scope:	indexes the full text of the following services: NCSA What's New, NCSA Starting Points, W3 Virtual Library, ALIWEB, Yanoff's Special Internet Connections List, Gibbs' List of Multimedia Information Sources, December's List of Computer-Mediated Communication Information Sources, Speh's User Documents
Volume:	n/a
Searching Tips:	unless you're a programmer and can understand the explanation of how to enter Perl regular expressions, your searching flexibility will be limited; queries with multiple keywords separated by spaces result in the intersection (Boolean "AND") of the keywords; try using only one keyword; if no hits are returned, try a related keyword; if too many hits are returned, add a related term to narrow the search
Strengths:	provides a full text search interface to some very popular and useful resources
Weaknesses:	a poorly documented query interface; slow response time
Updates:	daily
Questions:	scgwww@iam.unibe.ch
Submissions:	users must make submissions to the source databases, not to the CUI W3 Catalog

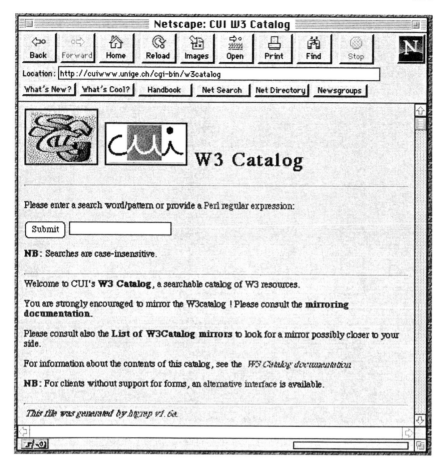

Figure 7–3   CUI's World Wide Web Catalog

Description

CUI W3 Catalog is a searchable full text index of several of the most popular and useful Internet virtual libraries and directories. Users may enter single or multiple keyword queries. Multiple keyword queries result in the intersection (Boolean "AND") of the keywords, which must be separated by spaces. Users familiar with the use of Perl regular expressions may enter more complex queries. See Appendix II.

Evaluation

Because each of the indexed services impose limitations on the length and content of resource descriptions, the resulting concatenated catalog possesses a reasonable degree of consistency with respect to resource description content and format. Because of this underlying structure, the database is of relatively high quality and query results can be displayed in a consistent structured manner. However, because the CUI W3 Catalog depends upon the currency of resources which are semi-automated or even wholly managed by people, it is not as up to date or comprehensive as many of the other search tools. In addition, the query interface is relatively inflexible and user-unfriendly. Despite these problems, the CUI

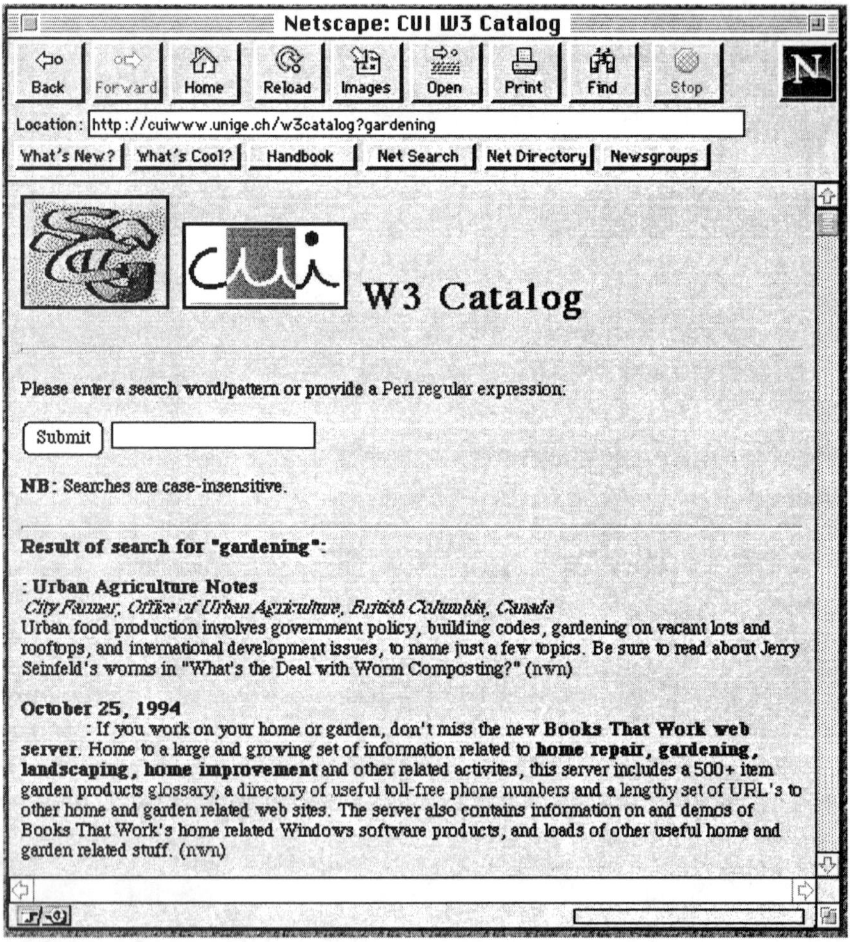

Figure 7–4   Results of a Sample Query Using the CUI W3 Catalog

W3 Catalog is a very popular resource, and thereby suffers from excessive slowness caused by too many people trying to use it. Mirror sites do exist and are often faster than the main site.

Sample Search

Objective: Lou is looking for some information about gardening and landscaping.

Lou begins his search by entering the keywords "gardening landscaping" into the query box. After submitting his query, Lou waits about a minute for the results. No matching entries are found. Lou tries again using only "gardening" as the keyword and is rewarded with three hits, one of which looks very promising.

DOMAIN NAME SEARCH TOOL

Meta Information

URL:	http://ibc.wustl.edu/domain_form.html
Resource Type:	World Wide Web site
Use:	finding domain names for organizations; finding URLs for the Web and Gopher sites of organizations; can be very useful if the domain name for a particular organization is not intuitive
Navigation:	keyword searches using words drawn from the organization's name and location
Scope:	domain names and in some cases Web and Gopher servers
Volume:	all domain names
Searching Tips:	use the least common word in the organization's name; follow that by one word from the state's name and one word from the city's name; if you get a really long list, try a more specific search or use the built-in search capability of your Web browser
Strengths:	the database of domain names is comprehensive and current
Weaknesses:	very little information is included in each record, which can make searching a challenge
Updates:	daily
Questions:	Hugh Chou, hugh@ibc.wustl.edu
Submissions:	domain names are indexed automatically

Description

This tool allows users to look up domain names of organizations using the name and location of that organization as the keywords. These keywords must be entered in the following order: *1: keyword from organization's name; 2: keywords from organization's location.* Users are searching a database of records that looks like this:

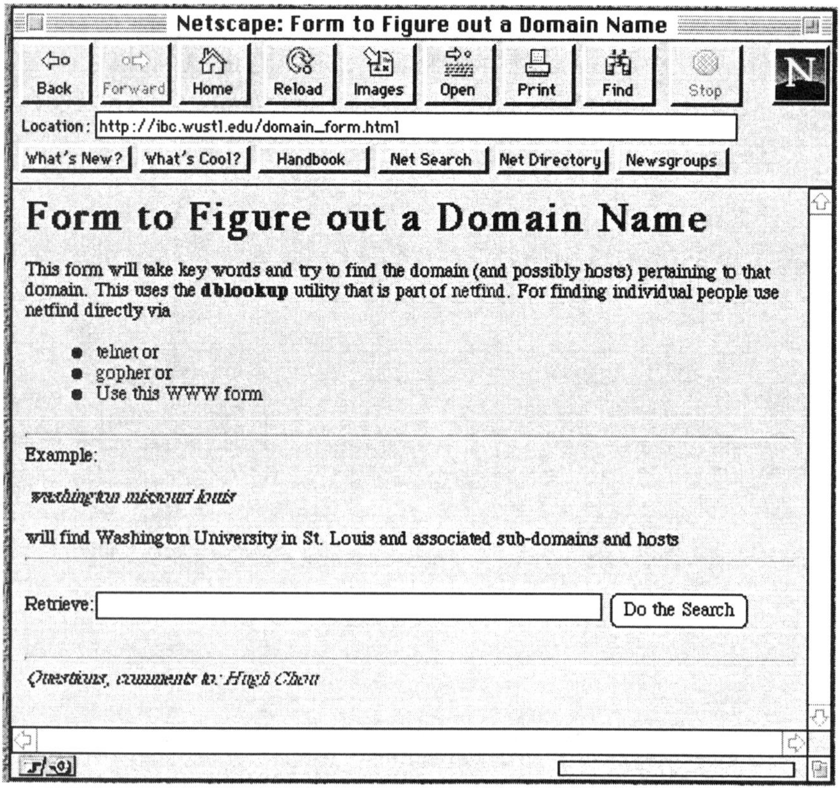

Figure 7–5   Domain Name Search Tool from Washington University

Domain: umi.com
Location: university microfilms, inc, ann arbor, michigan

This domain name lookup tool will sometimes also provide you with the URL for the organization's Gopher or Web server. This tool uses the dblookup utility that is part of NetFind. For people who are looking for individuals rather than organizations, it also provides several interfaces to NetFind.

Evaluation

If you need to find the domain name of a particular company, this tool can be very helpful. It is easy to use and responds quickly to queries. The interface could be designed better. The query box is at the bottom of the screen, rather than at the top. Also, the instructions are not as explicit as they could be. All in all, this is a good tool for performing a specific type of query.

Sample Search

Objective: Susan would like to find the URL for Argus Associates. She's tried http://argus.com with no luck. She knows that Argus is located in Ann Arbor, Michigan.

Susan enters the keywords "argus michigan arbor" and begins the search. The results show the domain name to be "argus-inc.com". Susan guesses (correctly) that the URL for the Argus Web site is http://argus-inc.com.

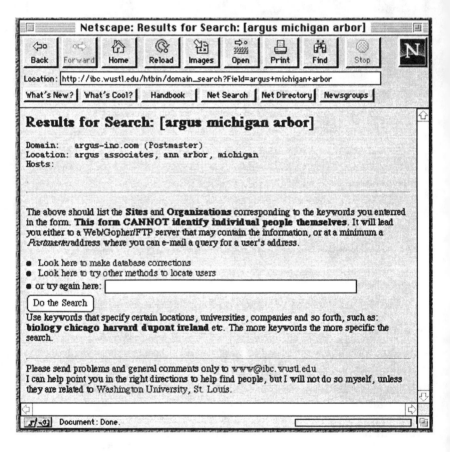

Figure 7–6   Results of a Domain Name Search

HARVEST

Meta Information

URL:	http://www.town.hall.org/brokers/www-home-pages/query.html
Resource Type:	World Wide Web site
Use:	finding information; finding top level "home pages"; useful for research and reference
Navigation:	perform keyword searching on author, keyword, title, and URL of resources; Boolean and adjacency searching are also supported
Scope:	broad; World Wide Web sites
Volume:	45,000 Web pages
Searching Tips:	start with a couple of keywords; if you receive too many hits, take advantage of the Boolean and adjacency search capabilities
Strengths:	a simple yet very powerful query interface; a fast search engine; well formatted display of search results
Weaknesses:	a relatively small database
Updates:	daily
Questions:	harvest-dvl@cs.colorado.edu
Submissions:	http://harvest.cs.colorado.edu/Harvest/brokers/register-with-CU-gatherers.html

Description

The Harvest WWW Home Pages Broker is a tool for searching through an indexed database of "home pages." A simple query box provides the user with the ability to perform keyword or fielded searching. The searchable database includes the author, keyword, title, and URL of each resource. Harvest supports Boolean and adjacency searching. For each matching resource, Harvest displays a hyperlinked URL, the host and path name, and the title. Results can be presented in a list, ranked according to the WAIS relevance ranking algorithm. The user can adjust the result set options.

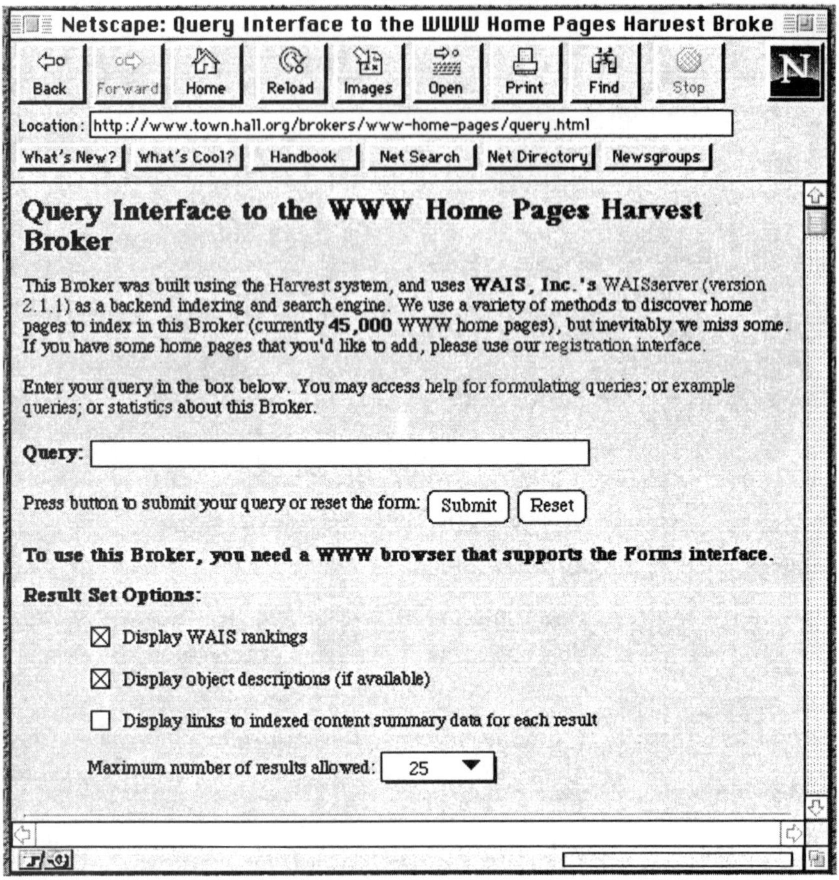

```
┌─────────────────────────────────────────────────────────────────────┐
│ ▓▒▓ Netscape: Query Interface to the WWW Home Pages Harvest Broke ▓█ │
├─────────────────────────────────────────────────────────────────────┤
│  ⟵○    ○⟶    ⌂      ⊗     🗐    ⇨○    ⊟     ⚇     ◎      │   N  │
│  Back  Forward Home  Reload Images Open  Print  Find  Stop   │      │
├─────────────────────────────────────────────────────────────────────┤
│ Location: │http://www.town.hall.org/brokers/www-home-pages/query.html││
├─────────────────────────────────────────────────────────────────────┤
│ What's New? │ What's Cool? │ Handbook │ Net Search │ Net Directory│ Newsgroups│
├─────────────────────────────────────────────────────────────────────┤
```

Query Interface to the WWW Home Pages Harvest Broker

This Broker was built using the Harvest system, and uses **WAIS, Inc.**'s WAISserver (version 2.1.1) as a backend indexing and search engine. We use a variety of methods to discover home pages to index in this Broker (currently **45,000** WWW home pages), but inevitably we miss some. If you have some home pages that you'd like to add, please use our registration interface.

Enter your query in the box below. You may access help for formulating queries; or example queries; or statistics about this Broker.

Query: [   ]

Press button to submit your query or reset the form: [Submit] [Reset]

To use this Broker, you need a WWW browser that supports the Forms interface.

Result Set Options:

☒ Display WAIS rankings

☒ Display object descriptions (if available)

☐ Display links to indexed content summary data for each result

Maximum number of results allowed: [25 ▼]

Figure 7–7   The Harvest WWW Home Pages Broker

Evaluation

Since Harvest only indexes the top levels of Web site hierarchies, searches tend to result in more useful sets of resources than are found with some of the other search tools. The query interface is simple but very flexible. The combination of free text searching with relevance ranking and Boolean and adjacency searching capabilities makes Harvest one of the more powerful search tools. However, the database is rather small when compared with some of the leading search tools. If you're looking for a few good resources on a particular topic Harvest is a great tool to use, but if you hope to conduct a fairly exhaustive search you will need to employ some of the other top search tools.

Sample Search

Objective: Garth is looking for the lyrics to popular country music songs.

Garth begins by entering "country and music and lyrics" as his query. Harvest returns a ranked list of hits. For each resource, a hyperlinked URL, host and path name, and title are provided.

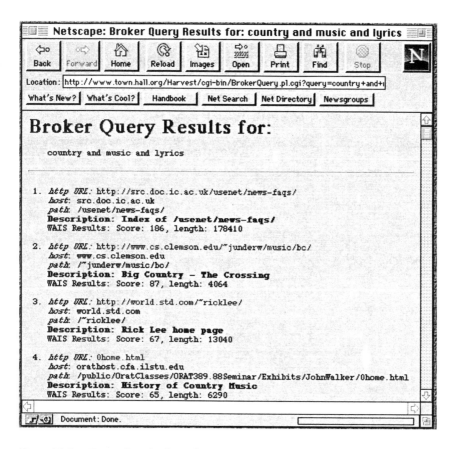

Figure 7–8   Query Results for a Sample Search

INFOSEEK

Meta Information

URL:	http://www.infoseek.com:80/Home
Resource Type:	World Wide Web site
Use:	finding information resources and services, software, and on-line communities; useful as both a research and reference tool
Navigation:	search using keywords and phrases; the minus sign (-) may be used as a NOT operator; restrictions may be placed on currency of resources and databases to be searched
Scope:	very broad; largest full text index of Web pages available; Usenet news full text index; several commercial databases
Volume:	Web index is over 1.5 gigabytes; Usenet index contains full text of past four weeks of over 10,000 newsgroups
Searching Tips:	given the immense size of the databases, be sure to enter very specific queries; read the on-line documentation carefully
Strengths:	the largest index of Web pages and Usenet news postings available; an excellent query interface with a very fast search engine
Weaknesses:	users must pay a combination of monthly and per search charges
Updates:	daily
Questions:	http://www.infoseek.com:80/Feedback
Submissions:	www-request@infoseek.com

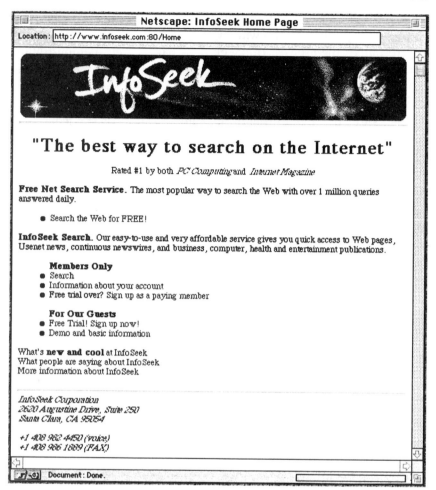

Figure 7–9   InfoSeek: Rated #1 by both *PC Computing* and *Internet Magazine*. InfoSeek is a registered trademark and the InfoSeek logo and Personal Newswire are trademarks of InfoSeek Corporation. Copyright 1994, 1995 InfoSeek Corporations. All rights reserved.

Description

InfoSeek is an Internet search tool that allows users to query relatively comprehensive databases of Web pages and Usenet news postings. Unlike most of the other tools and resources reviewed in this book, InfoSeek costs money to use. Pricing options include several combinations of monthly fees and per search charges. Users may choose to search the Web index and/or the Usenet index. Other commercial databases are also available. Complex searches can be constructed using Boolean logic and nested queries. Date ranges may also be specified. Results are presented as a list of hyperlinked titles with brief descriptions that are pulled from the resources themselves. InfoSeek does have a free "demonstration" search capability which is at least as useful as many of the other free Internet search tools. Searching is limited to the Web index, the interface is less flexible and user-friendly, and the number of hits is restricted to ten. A free one-month trial of the commercial grade service is available to all users who register.

Evaluation

InfoSeek's commercial grade service is the best Web and Usenet search tool available. The databases are far more comprehensive than those of most other tools, the query interface provides power and flexibility while remaining easy to use, and the search engine is very fast. The free "demonstration" service, while not nearly as powerful, still ranks among the most useful Internet search tools. The obvious downside to the commercial service is that it costs money. However, the fees are very fair and the pricing structure flexible enough to suit most types of searchers. As with all search tools, the quality of the indexed resources varies substantially and the presentation of results is relatively unorganized. In summary, InfoSeek is one of the best Internet research and reference tools available. Anyone who is serious about searching the Internet should at least try it out.

Sample Search

Objective: Hillary wants to know what people are talking about with respect to her health care policy.

Hillary enters "health-care-policy" into the query box and selects the most recent week of the Usenet news database. The hyphens indicate that the keywords must be adjacent. The results include several recent Usenet postings on the topic. Hillary decides to find some background information about health care in general, so she selects the Web page index and runs "health care" as her query. This time she gets a list of over 40 Web sites.

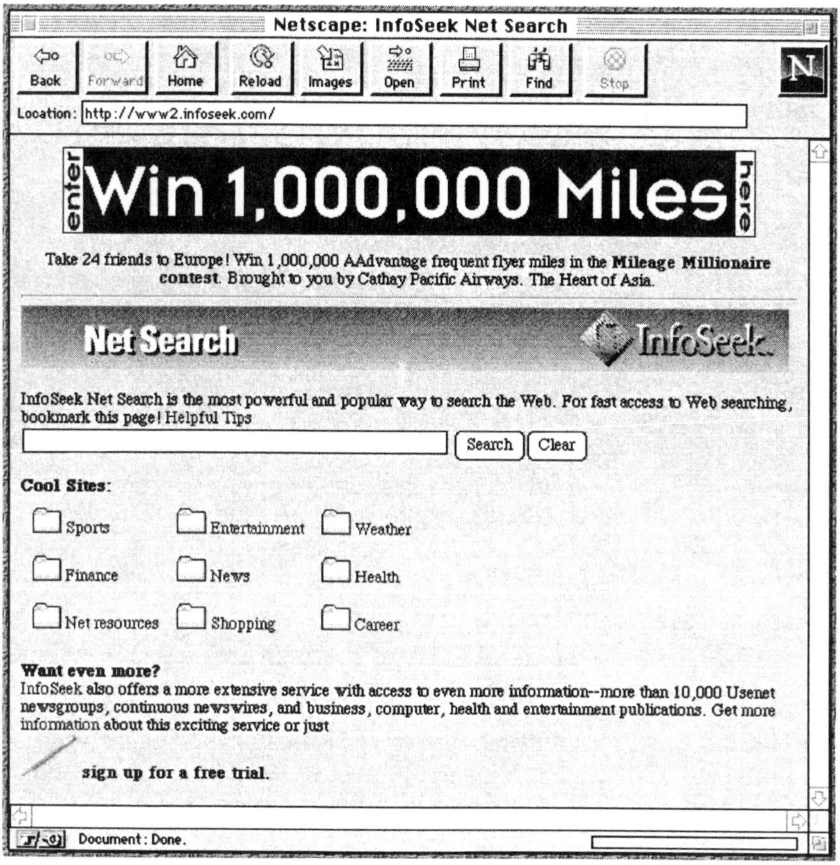

Figure 7–10 InfoSeek's Free Net Search Interface

JUMPSTATION II

Meta Information

URL:	http://js.stir.ac.uk/jsbin/jsii
Resource Type:	World Wide Web site
Use:	finding Web-based information resources and software and domain names; primarily useful as a re-search tool
Navigation:	search for documents by title, header, or subject; search for domain names by partial address
Scope:	very broad; Web document titles, headers, full text, and domain names
Volume:	n/a
Searching Tips:	for a narrow search, try restricting your query to the title field; for a more exhaustive search, include the subject field
Strengths:	ability to search on title, header, or subject provides substantial flexibility; an easy to use query interface; the search engine is fairly quick
Weaknesses:	the database is less comprehensive than those of several other search tools; updated on a very irregular basis
Updates:	highly variable
Questions:	Jonathon Fletcher, jonathon@japan.sbi.com
Submissions:	http://js.stir.ac.uk/jsbin/submit

Description

JumpStation is a tool for searching through the titles, headers, and full text of Web documents. Data for the JumpStation database is acquired by a "Net Robot" that traverses the World Wide Web's hypertext links in search of new documents to index. Query boxes are provided for title, header, and subject searches. Users may query any combination of these fields. Results are presented as hyperlinked URLs followed by document title, date of last modification, size in bytes, type (text, HTML, etc.) and

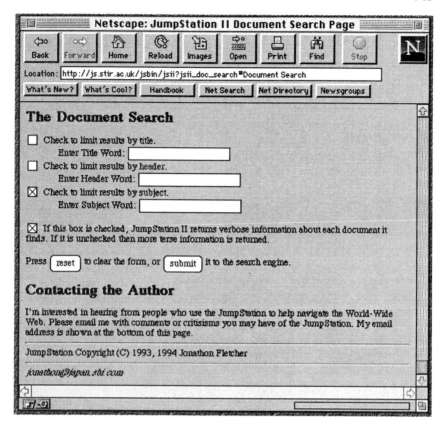

Figure 7–11   JumpStation II Document Search Page. Copyright 1993, 1994 by Jonathon Fletcher.

number of links. JumpStation also provides the capability to search for domain names. A user must enter a partial domain name and JumpStation will use pattern matching to find the full name.

Evaluation

The intuitive interface, the ability to restrict queries to the title field, and the fast response time combine to make JumpStation a good tool to use for quick searches of the Web. The query results screen is nicely formatted and the presentation of meta information about each resource (date of last modification, size in bytes, type (text, HTML, etc.) and number of links) is an unusual and interesting feature. On the downside, the database is far from comprehensive and is not kept up to date.

Sample Search

Objective: Norm wants information about health and fitness pro-
                    grams.

Norm begins his search by using "health" as the keyword in the "subject"
field. This initial search returns dozens of documents, many of which are
not useful. Norm decides to narrow his search by restricting the query to
the "title" field. This time less than a dozen hits are returned, most of
them related to the topic of health and fitness.

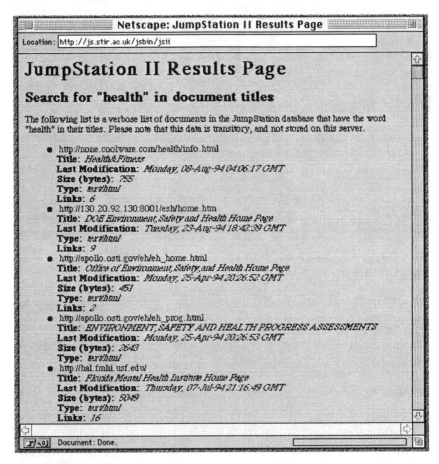

Figure 7–12   The JumpStation II Results Page. Copyright 1993, 1994 by Jonathon
Fletcher.

LYCOS

Meta Information

URL:	http://wpw.lycos.com/
Resource Type:	World Wide Web site
Use:	finding Internet information resources and services, software, and on-line communities; useful as both a research and reference tool
Navigation:	search the full text of Web, Gopher, and FTP resources; hits are given a score and ordered based on a relevance ranking algorithm
Scope:	very broad; includes Web, Gopher, and FTP resources
Volume:	over five million unique URLs
Searching Tips:	use a period after keywords (e.g., library.) to force an exact match; use a hyphen before a keyword (e.g., -academic) to reduce the score of documents containing that keyword
Strengths:	one of the most comprehensive indices of Internet resources; an intuitive query interface
Weaknesses:	so popular that search requests are often denied
Updates:	weekly
Questions:	webmaster@www.lycos.com
Submissions:	http://www.lycos.com/register.html

Description

Lycos is a tool that indexes the full text of Internet resources and then provides access via a fairly intuitive query interface and a powerful search engine. Resources are acquired for the database by the Lycos "spider robot" that traverses the Internet in search of new resources. Users may add resources which have not been discovered by the spider. The Lycos search form allows users to perform free text queries. Users may input several keywords separated by spaces. Advanced searchers may use periods to force exact matches and hyphens to produce negative indicatives

Figure 7–13   Lycos: The Catalog of the Internet. Copyright 1995 Lycos, Inc. All rights reserved.

(these keywords will have a negative effect on the document ranking). Results are presented as a ranked list of hits with hyperlinked URLs, file length in bytes, numbers of links, title, an outline or brief excerpt, and several keywords.

Evaluation

Lycos is an award winning tool for finding Internet information. The Lycos database is one of the most comprehensive in existence. The intuitive query interface and the relevance ranking algorithm combine to make Lycos a very easy tool to use. At the same time, the advanced query capabilities provide the flexibility that experienced searchers desire. The ability to restrict the display of results to a terse output is a nice feature. On the downside, Lycos' popularity creates frequent bottlenecks that prevent users from submitting queries or slow down queries that have been entered. Lycos also suffers from the fact that the indexed resources vary substantially in terms of quality. Finally, the fuzzy nature of the relevance ranking scheme makes it impossible to conduct exact searches. Overall, despite these problems, Lycos is one of the best search tools on the Internet.

Figure 7–14   Lycos Search Form. Copyright 1995 Lycos Inc. All rights reserved.

Sample Search

Objective: Norm is looking for a new place to drink beer and eat food in Boston.

From the search form interface, Norm enters "beer boston restaurant" into the query box. He then raises the maximum number of hits to five and the minimum number of terms required for a match to three. This means that no more than five documents will be displayed in the result set and all three of the keywords must be present in the document for a match. Lycos indicates that it found 18,209 documents matching at least one search term and then presents the 25 highest ranked documents. The first ranked hit is the Boston Restaurant List which provides all of the information Norm is looking for.

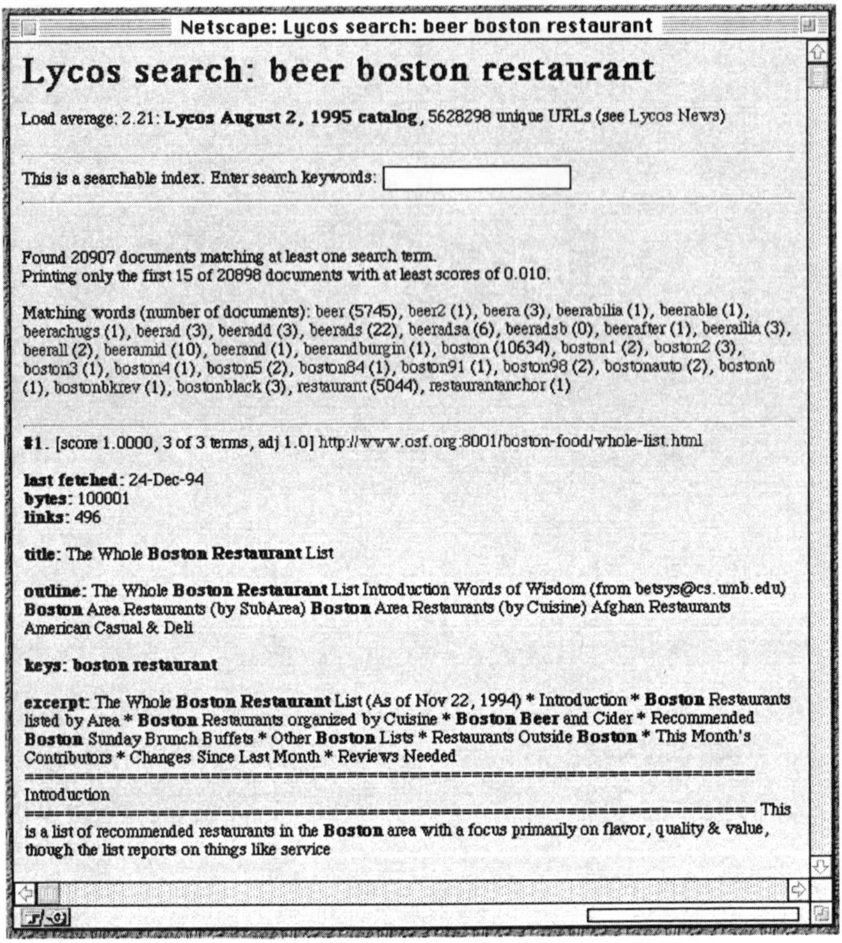

Netscape: Lycos search: beer boston restaurant

Lycos search: beer boston restaurant

Load average: 2.21: **Lycos August 2, 1995 catalog**, 5628298 unique URLs (see Lycos News)

This is a searchable index. Enter search keywords: [   ]

Found 20907 documents matching at least one search term.
Printing only the first 15 of 20898 documents with at least scores of 0.010.

Matching words (number of documents): beer (5745), beer2 (1), beera (3), beerabilia (1), beerable (1), beerachugs (1), beerad (3), beeradd (3), beerads (22), beeradsa (6), beeradsb (0), beerafter (1), beerailia (3), beerall (2), beeramid (10), beerand (1), beerandburgin (1), boston (10634), boston1 (2), boston2 (3), boston3 (1), boston4 (1), boston5 (2), boston84 (1), boston91 (1), boston98 (2), bostonauto (2), bostonb (1), bostonbkrev (1), bostonblack (3), restaurant (5044), restaurantanchor (1)

#1. [score 1.0000, 3 of 3 terms, adj 1.0] http://www.osf.org:8001/boston-food/whole-list.html

last fetched: 24-Dec-94
bytes: 100001
links: 496

title: The Whole **Boston Restaurant** List

outline: The Whole **Boston Restaurant** List Introduction Words of Wisdom (from betsys@cs.umb.edu) **Boston** Area Restaurants (by SubArea) **Boston** Area Restaurants (by Cuisine) Afghan Restaurants American Casual & Deli

keys: boston restaurant

excerpt: The Whole **Boston Restaurant** List (As of Nov 22, 1994) * Introduction * **Boston** Restaurants listed by Area * **Boston** Restaurants organized by Cuisine * **Boston Beer** and Cider * Recommended **Boston** Sunday Brunch Buffets * Other **Boston** Lists * Restaurants Outside **Boston** * This Month's Contributors * Changes Since Last Month * Reviews Needed
==
Introduction
== This
is a list of recommended restaurants in the **Boston** area with a focus primarily on flavor, quality & value, though the list reports on things like service

---

Figure 7–15   Results of a Lycos Search. Copyright 1995 Lycos, Inc. All rights reserved.

NLIGHTN

Meta Information

URL:	http://www.nlightn.com/
Resource Type:	World Wide Web site
Use:	finding Internet information resources and services, software, and on-line communities; useful as both a research and reference tool
Navigation:	search the full text of Web, Gopher, and FTP resources
Scope:	very broad
Volume:	over five million unique URLs (uses the Lycos index)
Searching Tips:	given the size of the database, it's a good idea to use more than one keyword; separate multiple keywords with spaces
Strengths:	very large database
Weaknesses:	searching can be slow; results are not presented in manner that facilitates rapid scanning
Updates:	weekly
Questions:	help@nlightn.com
Submissions:	n/a

Description

NlightN provides access to the immense Lycos index of World Wide Web sites. Users may keyword search the full text of over five million documents. NlightN also allows users to search commercial databases and news services. However, retrieval of documents from these commercial sources costs money. The searching interface is a simple query box and results are presented as a list of titles. By selecting the title, users can view the Lycos abstract for a particular resource and then visit the resource itself.

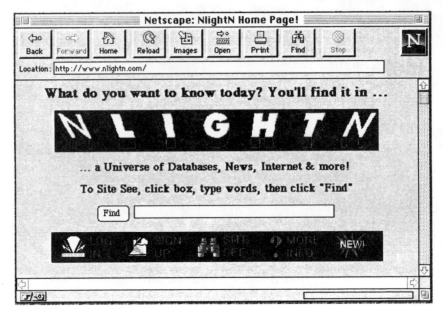

Figure 7–16   NlightN

Evaluation

NlightN provides an alternative means of accessing the Lycos index. Since Lycos is often so busy that connections are refused, NlightN is a useful backup. The query interface is very basic and provides no instructions regarding the execution of more complex queries. This is a major problem when searching such a large database. Also, the results display is not well presented and makes it difficult to scan through the listings for useful resources. Finally, searching the NlightN database can be very slow.

Sample Search

Objective: Rosalind is interested in starting up an ostrich ranch and would like to find as much information on the topic as possible.

Rosalind enters "ostrich" as her keyword and selects the Internet index. She browses through the long list of results and selects the "Get" button to view abstracts from resources that look promising.

OPEN TEXT WEB INDEX

Meta Information

URL:	http://www.opentext.com:8080/omw.html
Resource Type:	World Wide Web site
Use:	finding information resources, services, and software on the Web; useful as both a research and reference tool
Navigation:	search the full texts, titles, headings, URLs and hyperlinks of Web documents; use Boolean logic (AND, OR, BUT NOT, NEAR, FOLLOWED BY); rank query terms
Scope:	Web documents
Volume:	n/a
Searching Tips:	for a simple search, just enter a couple of terms; for a more complex search, use the "compound" search form which allows you to perform field specific queries and use Boolean logic
Strengths:	one of the best query interfaces available; the simple query interface is as easy to use as they come, while the compound query interface provides more power and flexibility than any other Internet search tool; very fast response time
Weaknesses:	a smaller database than that used by some of the other search tools
Updates:	daily
Questions:	webindex@opentext.com
Submissions:	http://www.opentext.com:8080/omw-submit.html

Description

The Open Text Web Index is a relatively new tool for searching the Web. Open Text supports simple keyword searches via a typical query box, or more complex compound queries via a query builder. Users can also rank the query terms in order of importance. A number of pre-determined "hot" searches are also available. In addition, once a useful document has

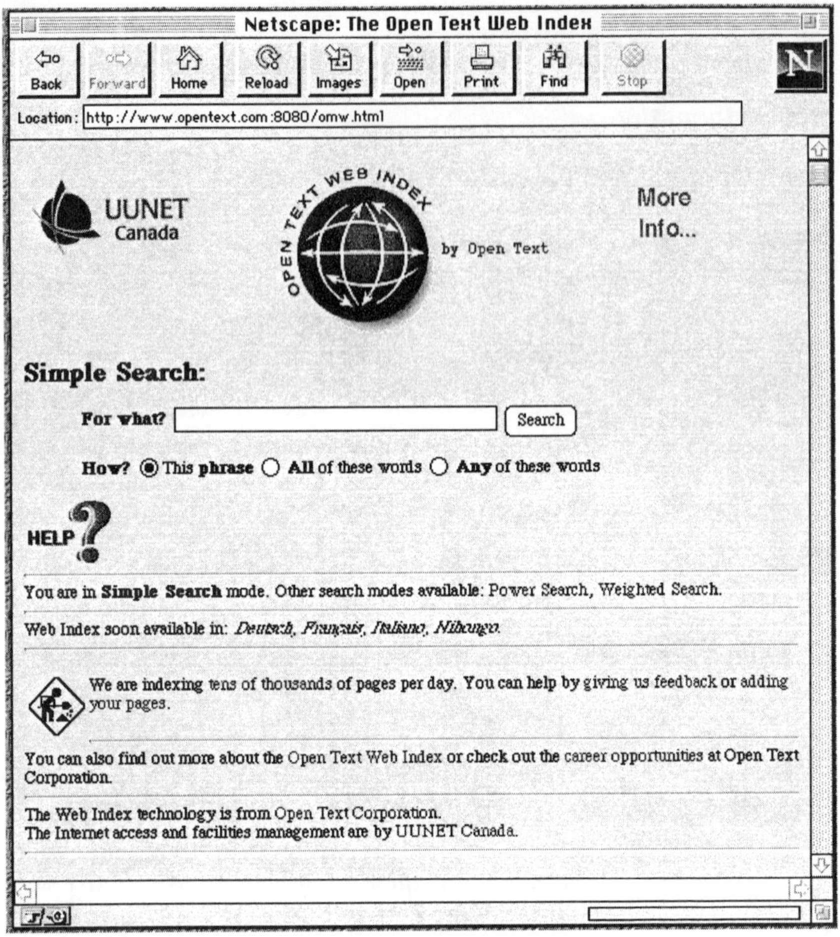

Figure 7–17   Open Text Web Index: Simple Search Interface

been discovered, users can ask the Web Index to "find similar pages."
Results are presented with a hyperlinked title, the file size and number
of matches in the document, and the URL. Users may go to the resource,
view sample matches in context, or find similar pages. Open Text displays
ten hits at a time and provides the option to view the next ten hits.

Evaluation

The Open Text Web Index possesses one of the best query interfaces
available on the Web. The Open Text search engine is very powerful,
flexible, and fast. By combining field specific searching, Boolean logic
capabilities, term weighting and relevance feedback features, Open Text
has developed a very useful tool. While the database is not currently as

extensive as those used by Lycos and InfoSeek, Open Text is indexing "tens of thousands of pages per day." As this index comes up to par, you can expect Open Text to become one of the most popular search tools on the Internet.

Sample Search

Objective: Carla would like to find some information about African culture. She is not interested in African-American culture for the purposes of this search.

Carla decides to use the compound search form. She enters "african" in the first query box, selects "and" as the first Boolean operator and enters "culture" and then selects "but not" as the second Boolean operator, and then enters "american" in the second query box. This search returns over

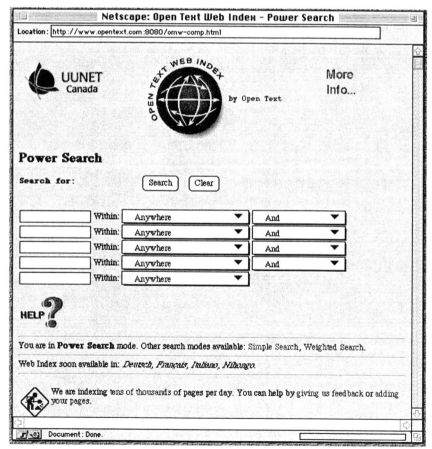

Figure 7–18   Open Text Web Index: Power Search

520 hits, many of which are false drops. Carla returns to the search form and limits "african" and "culture" to the title field. This more specific search returns only five hits, all of which look very promising.

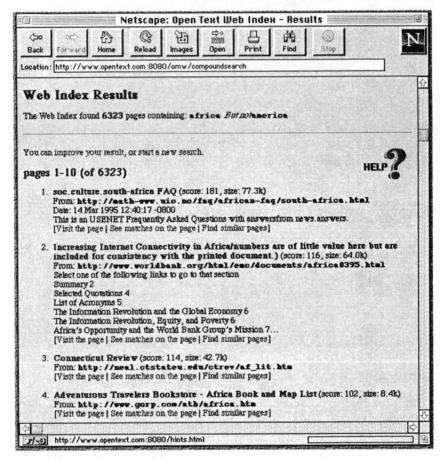

Figure 7–19   Web Index Results

POINT

Meta Information

URL:	http://www.pointcom.com/
Resource Type:	World Wide Web site
Use:	finding high quality Web sites; more useful for reference than research
Navigation:	search the database of site descriptions; browse the reviews of top ten sites in the following categories: most visited, top content, top presentation, top experience, top site hall of fame
Scope:	descriptions of the top Web sites as rated by the Point staff
Volume:	more than 5,000 Web sites
Searching Tips:	the best way to navigate is via the "Point Search" keyword search interface; enter two or three relevant keywords to take advantage of the relevance ranking algorithm
Strengths:	excellent resource descriptions; ability to search only on descriptions produces high searching precision
Weaknesses:	relatively small database; rather confusing interface for browsing
Updates:	weekly
Questions:	webmaster@point.com
Submissions:	http://www.pointcom.com/text/submit/

Description

Point is a searchable index of descriptions and evaluations of the top five percent of Web sites, as rated by the Point staff. A keyword search returns a ranked list of Web site titles. A description and evaluation is provided for each site. Sites are given a numerical evaluation for level of content, presentation, and experience. Users can also browse through the database of descriptions by selecting "Survey Web Reviews." The reviews are divided into 15 top level categories.

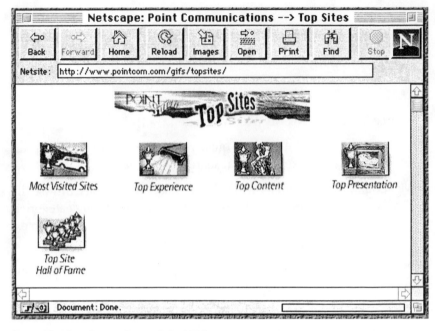

Figure 7–20   Point: Best of the Web

Evaluation

If you're looking for some high quality Web sites on a particular topic, Point can be a great place to start looking. The resource descriptions and evaluations make it easy to select interesting sites. The search engine is fast and the relevance ranking helps to sift through the database. The major problem with Point is the limited size of the database. By reviewing only five percent of existing Web sites, Point is far from comprehensive. Also, since users can only search the resource descriptions and not the full text of those sites, relevant Web sites can easily be missed. Finally, the browsing interface to Point is rather confusing. The textual homepage, for instance, is poorly organized. It's difficult to tell what capabilities are available without browsing through each category in turn.

Sample Search

Objective: Chris, an executive in the pharmaceutical industry is interested in finding out whether any competitors are using the Internet in innovative ways.

Chris selects the "search" function of Point and enters "pharmaceutical" as his keyword. Point returns a couple of hits and Chris selects one entitled "Warner-Lambert." Point provides an excellent description of the

Warner-Lambert site which leads Chris to explore the site itself. Chris decides to try browsing via the "Survey Web Reviews" option. He first selects "Science and Technology" but finds no corporate sites in that category. He then tries "Business and Finance" where he finds the "Companies" sub-category that includes all the reviews of corporate Web sites.

VERONICA GATEWAY

Meta Information

URL:	http://www.scs.unr.edu/veronica.html
Resource Type:	World Wide Web site
Use:	finding information resources, services, and software accessible via Gophers; most useful for research
Navigation:	keyword search the titles of files and directories of Gophers
Scope:	broad; includes most file and directory titles in Gopherspace; also includes some Web and FTP site references
Volume:	Ten million items from approximately 5,500 Gopher servers
Searching Tips:	begin by searching both file and directory titles; if you receive too many hits, try restricting the next search to only directory titles; for the more advanced searcher, Veronica does understand Boolean logic (AND, OR, NOT, parenthetical nesting); if you can't find what you're looking for, you might try a different Veronica server since the indices are not always consistent from server to server
Strengths:	ability to perform nested Boolean searching on document and/or menu titles
Weaknesses:	restricted to searching of Gophers' document and menu titles; often difficult to find a server that is not busy
Updates:	variable
Questions:	n/a
Submissions:	n/a

Description

Veronica is an index and retrieval tool for locating information resources on Gopher servers. Veronica allows users to search for keywords in document and menu titles. Veronica supports the use of Boolean operators (AND, OR, NOT) and allows nested queries through the use of parentheses. Veronica returns a hit list of document and/or menu titles. Each title is an active link to the resource itself. This gateway serves as an interface to several Veronica servers. The servers are divided into two categories; those that search document and menu titles and those that search only menu titles. Information about how to use Veronica is also provided.

Evaluation

On the bright side, Veronica is a fairly mature Internet search tool that provides a nice array of Boolean capabilities. However, Veronica and Gopher are essentially old technologies that have been superseded by

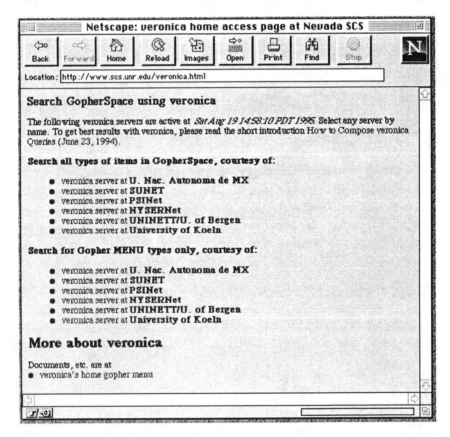

Figure 7–21　Veronica Gateway

the new generation of World Wide Web tools and resources. Relatively little information is being added to Gopherspace, so much of the information retrieved by Veronica is out of date. Since searching is limited to document and menu titles, it can be very difficult to find what you're looking for. Finally, the Veronica servers are often overloaded (which means they must still be popular) making it difficult to successfully submit a query. Overall, Veronica is a well developed tool whose time has passed.

Sample Search

Objective: Larry would like to find some information about an upcoming software management conference in San Francisco.

Larry decides to start with the "search menu and document titles" option and switch to the "search menus only" if he needs to narrow his search. He selects the Veronica server at PSINet, enters "software and management and conference and francisco" into the query box, and submits his query. The server replies with a "too many connections" message, so Larry tries one of the other Veronica servers. Finally, his query is successful and he is presented with a list of Gopher menu and document titles. He selects the ones that he finds most promising and soon finds the information he is looking for.

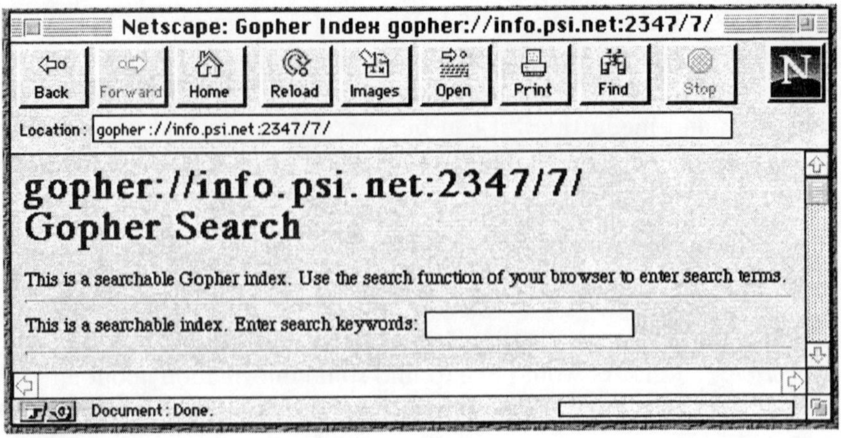

Netscape: Gopher Index gopher://info.psi.net:2347/7/

Back   Forward   Home   Reload   Images   Open   Print   Find   Stop

Location: gopher://info.psi.net:2347/7/

gopher://info.psi.net:2347/7/ Gopher Search

This is a searchable Gopher index. Use the search function of your browser to enter search terms.

This is a searchable index. Enter search keywords:

Document: Done.

Figure 7–22   Veronica's Query Interface

WAIS GATEWAY

Meta Information

URL:	http://www.wais.com/directory-of-servers.html
Resource Type:	World Wide Web site
Use:	finding information about very specific topics; searching archives of some e-mail discussion groups and Usenet newsgroups; useful for research and reference
Navigation:	search database abstracts to determine the correct databases; search the full text of document databases using natural language queries and Boolean and proximity commands
Scope:	detailed coverage of highly specific topics
Volume:	over 500 databases
Searching Tips:	begin by searching the directory of servers to identify potentially useful databases; use a few general keywords; once you have selected a few good databases, use more specific keywords to find what you're looking for; for Boolean and adjacency searching, read the "searching tips" section under the "help" menu.
Strengths:	if an individual or organization has taken the time to create a good WAIS database on the topic you're interested in, this can be a great place to search; the full text search engine and relevance ranking capabilities makes it very easy to search; response time is excellent
Weaknesses:	a limited number of topics are covered; the database abstracts do not always provide sufficient information to help users find an appropriate database; the quality, currency and type of information varies widely from database to database
Updates:	variable
Questions:	Webmaster@wais.com
Submissions:	n/a

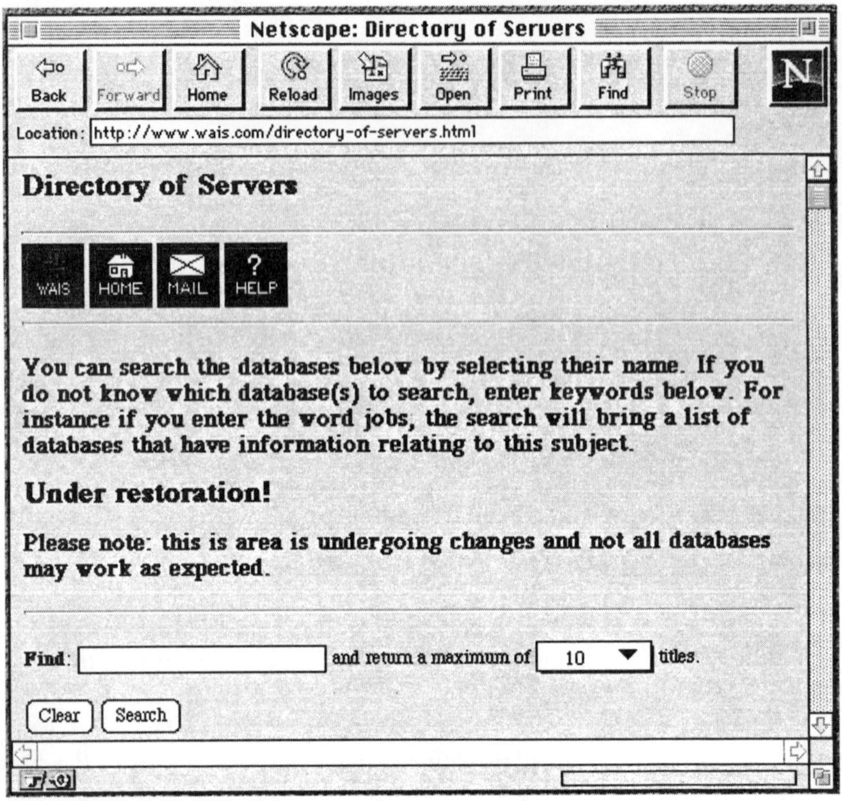

Figure 7–23   WAIS Gateway. Copyright © 1995 by America Online, Inc. Reprinted with permission.

Description

WAIS (Wide Area Information Server) is a tool that facilitates full text searching of distributed databases. These databases may be composed of abstracts, full text documents, or numerical data. Sample databases include aboriginal studies, the book of Mormon, genetic cloning, and poetry. Users select appropriate databases by querying the directory of servers, an index of database abstracts. After selecting a database, users may search the full text of that database by entering natural language queries. Boolean operators and an adjacency command may also be used. WAIS returns a list of document titles ranked according to a relevance ranking algorithm. Users may browse the list of hits and view the full text of selected documents.

Evaluation

Some of the WAIS databases are excellent resources and the full text searching capability of WAIS provides a fast and easy means of finding useful documents or data from within very large databases. With the addition of Boolean and adjacency searching capabilities, WAIS is even more flexible. However, good WAIS databases are relatively few in number. Many are out of date or of poor quality. Overall, WAIS is a great tool, but the content it accesses is rather limited.

Figure 7–24   Results of a Sample WAIS Search. Copyright © 1995 by America Online, Inc. Reprinted with permission.

Sample Search

Objective: Jen wants to find transcripts of exchanges between President Clinton and President Boris Yeltsin.

Jen begins her search with the directory of servers by entering "president" as her keyword. From the resulting list of databases, Jen selects the "White House Papers." This time Jen enters a more specific query, "clinton and yeltsin." She is rewarded by a ranked list of documents, many of which look very promising.

Figure 7–25   Wandex. Copyright © 1995 by America Online, Inc. Reprinted with permission.

WANDEX

Meta Information

URL:	http://www.netgen.com/cgi/wandex
Resource Type:	World Wide Web site
Use:	finding Web based information resources and services; useful primarily as a reference tool
Navigation:	keyword search the titles, URLs, descriptions, and keywords of Web sites; results displayed as ranked list
Scope:	very broad
Volume:	over 15,700 Web sites
Searching Tips:	try one or two keywords that you would expect to find in the titles of the resources you are looking for; if you don't find anything on the first search, try a few related keywords
Strengths:	fast search engine; relevance ranking of results
Weaknesses:	very basic search capabilities; a limited database; no descriptive or evaluative information presented in result set
Updates:	weekly
Questions:	Matthew Gray, mkgray@netgen.com
Submissions:	http://www.netgen.com/cgi/addhost

Description

Wandex is a World Wide Web index generated by the WWW Wanderer and the net.Index prototype, an autonomous content analysis-based search engine. Wandex indexes Web based information resources and services and allows basic keyword searching of titles, URLs, descriptions, and keywords. The results are presented as a list of titles and URLs, ordered according to a relevance ranking algorithm.

Evaluation

The query interface is straightforward and the search engine fairly fast. The presentation of results as a list of "best" and "good" hits is a nice feature. However, the search capabilities appear to be rather limited in terms of flexibility and the database is relatively small compared to those indexed by some of the more popular search tools.

Sample Search

Objective: Lara would like to find some information about the U.S. Fish and Wildlife Service.

Lara begins her search by entering "fish wildlife" into the query box. She is presented with a list of "Best Matches" and a list of "Good Matches." Both lists provide a hyperlinked title and a URL for each resource.

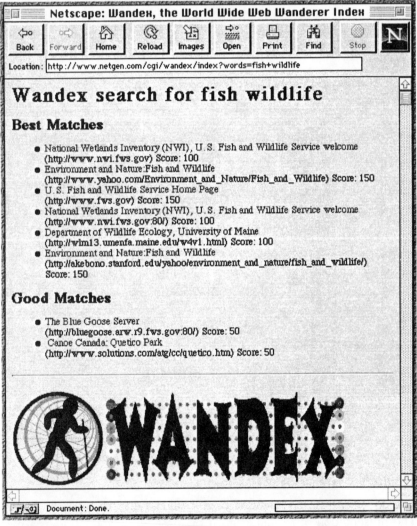

Figure 7–26   Results of a Sample Wandex Search

WEBCRAWLER

Meta Information

URL:	http://webcrawler.com/
Resource Type:	World Wide Web site
Use:	finding Internet information resources and services, software, and on-line communities; useful as both a research and reference tool
Navigation:	keyword search the titles and full texts of Web pages; Boolean (AND, OR) capability
Scope:	very broad
Volume:	over 59,000 Web sites
Searching Tips:	given the large size of the WebCrawler database, fairly specific searches are usually the most productive; make good use of the Boolean "and" option
Strengths:	a very well-designed query interface; one of the most comprehensive databases available; a fast search engine
Weaknesses:	no descriptive or evaluative information provided; quality and currency of indexed resources varies widely
Updates:	weekly
Questions:	info@webcrawler.com
Submissions:	http://webcrawler.com/WebCrawler/SubmitURLS.html

Description

WebCrawler is a tool for searching the Web. WebCrawler's robot operates by traversing the Web and building an index of the documents it finds. Users can also submit resources for indexing. Users search WebCrawler using keyword queries. Basic Boolean operators (AND, OR) may be employed. Users can also modify the number of results to be displayed. The result set is presented as a ranked list of hyperlinked document titles.

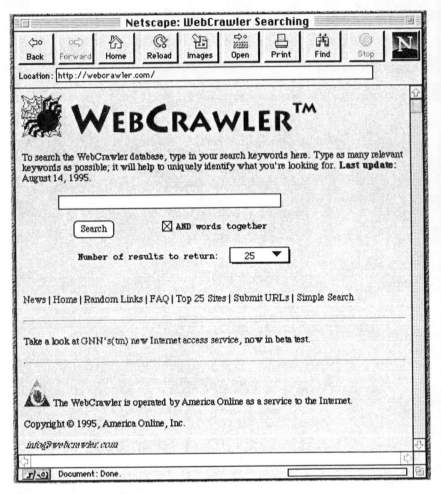

Figure 7–27   WebCrawler. Copyright 1995 America Online, Inc. All rights reserved.

Evaluation

WebCrawler is one of the best and most popular Internet searching tools. The query interface is one of the more elegant interfaces you will encounter. Searching is very easy for the beginner, but WebCrawler is a favorite tool of experts as well. The database is relatively comprehensive, yet searches are completed with blinding speed. On the down side, no descriptive or evaluative information is presented in the hit list. If you get a long list of results, it can be rather frustrating to check each link. Overall, WebCrawler is an excellent tool whether you're conducting exhaustive research or just trying to find the answer to a simple question.

Sample Search

Objective: Jake would like to find a recipe for pumpkin pie.

The default settings for WebCrawler queries are "AND words together" and "25" as the maximum number of results to display, so Jake simply enters "recipe pumpkin pie" and submits the query. He is rewarded by a ranked list of hyperlinked document titles. The second-ranked hit, a recipe index, looks very promising.

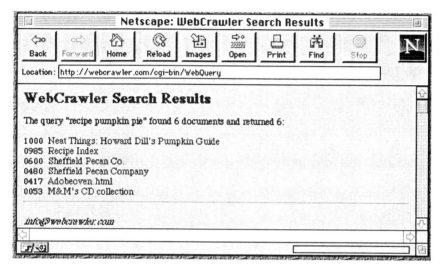

Figure 7–28 WebCrawler Results Page. Copyright 1995 America Online, Inc. All rights reserved.

WORLD WIDE WEB WORM

Meta Information

URL:	http://www.cs.colorado.edu/home/mcbryan/ WWW.html
Resource Type:	World Wide Web site
Use:	finding information resources and services, software, and on-line communities; useful as both a research and reference tool
Navigation:	keyword search URLs, URL references, and document titles; limited Boolean (AND, OR) searching capabilities
Scope:	very broad; Web sites
Volume:	over three million unique URLs
Searching Tips:	given the large size of the database, it's a good idea to begin with a fairly specific search; try searching only the document titles; make use of the Boolean "and"
Strengths:	excellent query and results display interfaces; one of the most comprehensive databases; a fast search engine
Weaknesses:	not as current as some of the other search tools
Updates:	irregular
Questions:	Oliver A. McBryan, mcbryan@cs.colorado.edu
Submissions:	http://www.cs.colorado.edu/home/mcbryan/ WWWWadd.html

Description

The W3 Worm is a tool for finding information resources and services on the World Wide Web. Searchable fields include URLs, URL references or hyperlinks within documents, and document titles. Users may use the Boolean operators (AND, OR) in conducting searches. Searches may be limited to a specific number of matches. Results are displayed as a list of hyperlinked titles.

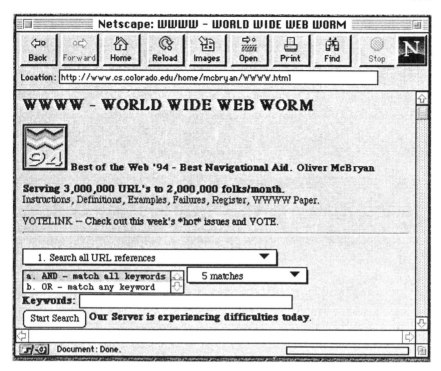

Figure 7–29 The World Wide Web Worm

Evaluation

It's no surprise that the W3 Worm won the title of "Best Navigational Aid" at "Best of the Web '94." W3 Worm provides a simple yet powerful interface for searching a large database of information. The ability to search only document titles combined with the use of Boolean operators allows the user to execute very specific queries. The search engine is very fast and results are displayed in a list of titles that is very easy to browse through. The only downside to the W3 Worm is that updating of the database seems to be done on a very irregular basis. Overall, W3 Worm is a great tool to use for conducting reference or research on the Internet.

Sample Search

Objective: Malcolm wants to find some information about molecular biology.

Malcolm begins by restricting his search to document titles. He selects the "AND - match all keywords" option and limits the display results to a maximum of 50 hits. Malcolm uses "molecular" and "biology" as his query terms. W3 Worm displays a list of hyperlinked titles that contain both keywords.

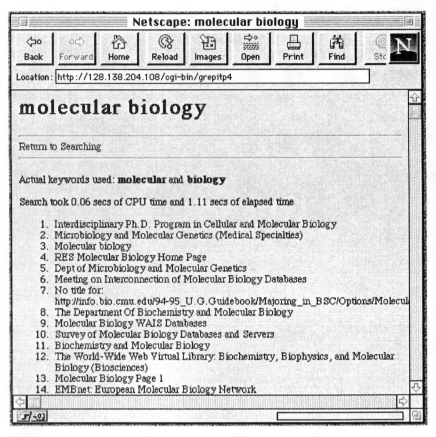

Figure 7–30   Query Results for the World Wide Web Worm

SEARCH FOR SOFTWARE

ARCHIEPLEX (NASA IMPLEMENTATION)

Meta Information

URL:	http://www.lerc.nasa.gov/Doc/archieplex.html also available from: http://hoohoo.ncsa.uiuc.edu/archie.html http://cuiwww.unige.ch/./archieplexform.html
Resource Type:	World Wide Web site
Use:	finding software files available via anonymous FTP; also finding documents and other files available via anonymous FTP
Navigation:	keyword search the file names (and in some cases descriptions) of software programs; limit results based on domain; order results alphabetically by host name or chronologically by date
Scope:	public domain software (shareware and freeware)
Volume:	tens of thousands of software files from over 2,000 FTP sites
Searching Tips:	remember that you're searching file names; use short keywords or abbreviations; you may need to try a few before being successful
Strengths:	if you're looking for free software, Archie is an excellent tool
Weaknesses:	keyword searching of file titles is very limiting
Updates:	weekly
Questions:	Guy Brooker, guy@jw.estec.esa.nl
Submissions:	n/a

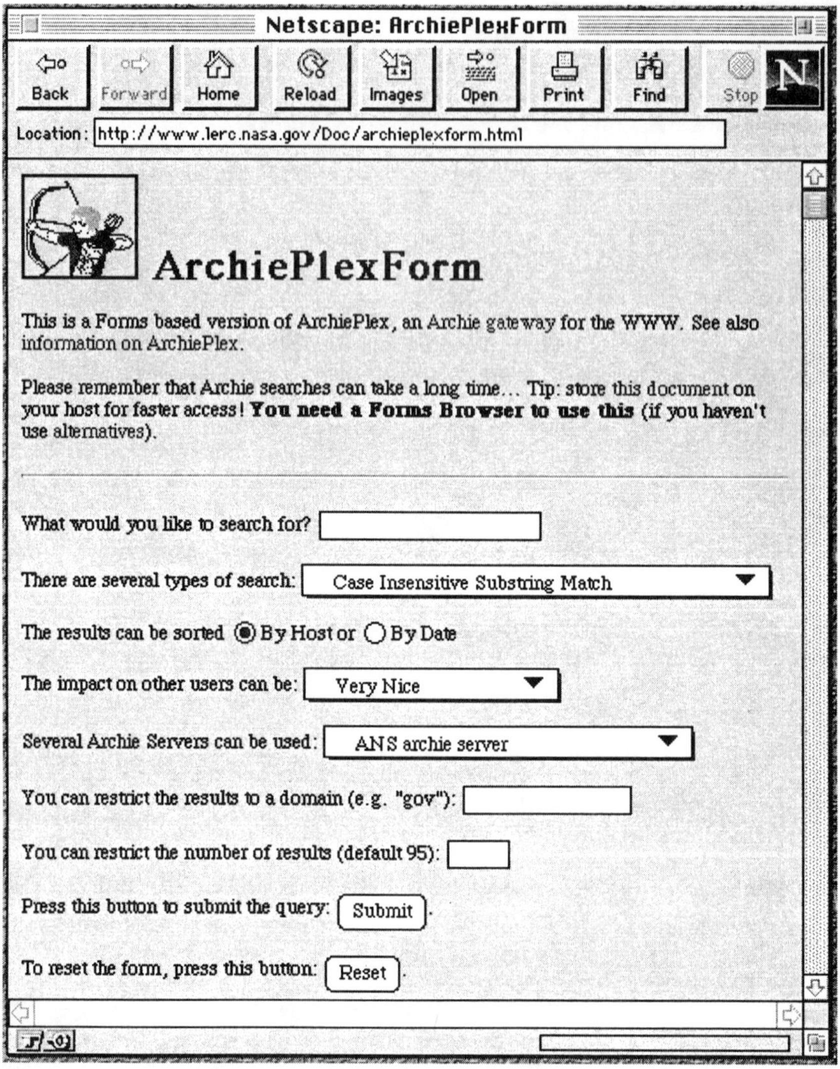

```
┌─────────────────────────────────────────────────────────────────┐
│ ▓▓▓□▓▓▓▓▓▓▓▓▓▓▓▓▓▓▓▓▓ Netscape: ArchiePlexForm ▓▓▓▓▓▓▓▓▓▓▓▓▓▓▓ │
├─────────────────────────────────────────────────────────────────┤
│  ⇦o    o⇨    ⌂     ◉     📷    ⇨o    ⊟     ⋕     ◎  N          │
│  Back  Forward Home  Reload  Images  Open  Print  Find   Stop     │
├─────────────────────────────────────────────────────────────────┤
│ Location: │http://www.lerc.nasa.gov/Doc/archieplexform.html │    │
└─────────────────────────────────────────────────────────────────┘
```

ArchiePlexForm

This is a Forms based version of ArchiePlex, an Archie gateway for the WWW. See also information on ArchiePlex.

Please remember that Archie searches can take a long time... Tip: store this document on your host for faster access! **You need a Forms Browser to use this** (if you haven't use alternatives).

What would you like to search for? [   ]

There are several types of search: [Case Insensitive Substring Match   ▼]

The results can be sorted ⦿ By Host or ◯ By Date

The impact on other users can be: [Very Nice   ▼]

Several Archie Servers can be used: [ANS archie server   ▼]

You can restrict the results to a domain (e.g. "gov"): [   ]

You can restrict the number of results (default 95): [   ]

Press this button to submit the query: [Submit].

To reset the form, press this button: [Reset].

Figure 7–31   ArchiePlex Form Interface

Description

Archie, one of the old guard of Internet searching tools, is used for finding software available for download on anonymous FTP archives. ArchiePlex is a forms-based World Wide Web interface to Archie. ArchiePlex allows you to search the file names of thousands of software files. Users can specify a "case insensitive substring match" or an "exact match." Results can be sorted alphabetically by host or chronologically by date. Users can restrict the search by domain or by numbers of hits to be displayed. Finally, users can select from a long list of Archie servers. If one server is busy, another one must be selected. The database of file names varies from server to server. Results are displayed as a list of hyperlinked host server names followed by hyperlinked folders followed by hyperlinked file names themselves. Files can be downloaded directly via a Web browser or indirectly via FTP client software.

Evaluation

If you're looking for software, Archie is the tool to use. It is by far the best developed tool dedicated to searching for software on the Internet. The ArchiePlex interface to Archie is well designed and eliminates the need for the arcane command syntax required by the text based Archie interfaces. However, ArchiePlex does not eliminate the underlying problem with Archie, namely the fact that the database is limited to file names. Searching is quite challenging to say the least. To make things worse, many of the Archie servers are frequently overloaded. Overall, Archie is an essential tool for finding software, but it can be frustrating to use.

Sample Search

Objective: Betsy wants to find the most recent version of Netscape to download.

Betsy uses "netscape" as the keyword and selects "sort by date" so that she can be sure to identify the most recent version. After submitting her query, she is rewarded with a list of servers with the Netscape software.

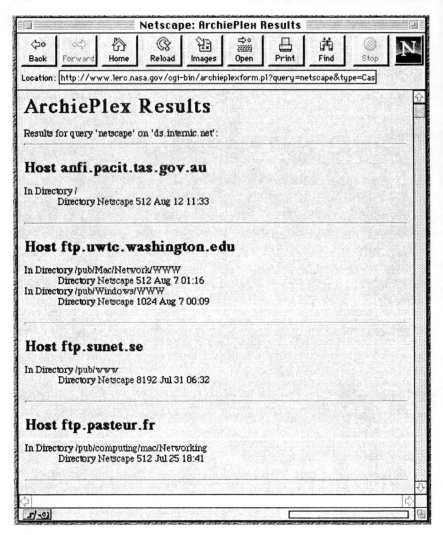

Figure 7–32   Results of a Sample Archie Search

VIRTUAL SOFTWARE LIBRARY

Meta Information

URL:	http://vsl.cnet.com/
Resource Type:	World Wide Web site
Use:	finding software files (shareware and freeware) available via anonymous FTP
Navigation:	keyword search the descriptions, file names, and directories of software applications; limit results by archive and date; sort files by date or path/directory
Scope:	public domain software (shareware and freeware)
Volume:	over 130,000 software programs
Searching Tips:	use the "Power Search" option which allows you to use Boolean logic (AND, NOT) and to search the file and path names; be flexible and persistent (you may need to try several keywords before finding what you need)
Strengths:	a terrific resource for finding software on the Internet; well-designed query interface; large database of file descriptions
Weaknesses:	file descriptions are very brief and often do not contain important keywords
Updates:	weekly
Questions:	managers@vsl.cnet.com
Submissions:	submit the software file to one of the archives indexed by VSL: http://vsl.cnet.com/cgi-bin/vsl-master/About

Description

The Virtual Software Library (VSL) allows you to search through the descriptions of more than 130,000 shareware and freeware programs that are stored on some of the largest anonymous FTP archives on the Internet. Shareware is software that you can try for free (authors request that you pay a registration fee if you decide to keep it). Freeware is totally free of charge. In addition to searching file descriptions, you can also use the "Power Search" option to search the file and path names. VSL provides the ability to use Boolean operators (AND, NOT). You can limit the number of hits to be displayed and the type of computer platform (e.g., MS-Windows, Macintosh, UNIX). Once you locate a file, you can read a brief description and download it directly from the archive.

Evaluation

The Virtual Software Library is the most powerful and user friendly tool available for searching the Internet's archives of shareware and freeware. After many slow, difficult, and often fruitless searches via Archie, VSL is a welcome addition to the suite of Internet search tools. The interface is well designed and makes it easy for users to take advantage of the various search options. Unfortunately, the descriptions provided by the software authors are often very short and do not include all of the relevant keywords. This places a real burden on the searcher. Overall, an excellent tool that takes the pain out of searching for software on the Internet.

Sample Search

Objective: Mike wants to find the "pkunzip.exe" program for decompressing file archives that have been compressed using "pkzip.exe".

Mike begins by selecting the "Power Search" option. He changes the "category of files to search" from MS-Windows to DOS. He uses "pkunzip" as his query term. Several descriptions of programs that relate to pkunzip are returned, but not the program Mike needs. He then tries searching the "specific directory/filename" for "pkunzip," again with no luck. Finally, Mike tries a search on "pk" and finds the program he needs. The file name is "pkz204g.exe" and the description is "PKWare ZIP archive create/extract pgm, v2.04g." Mike obviously had to be a fairly astute and persistent searcher to find this file.

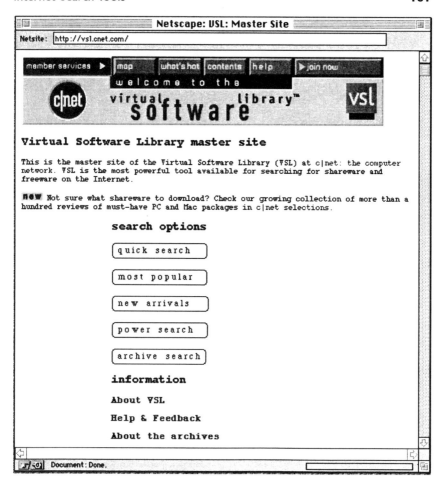

Figure 7–33   The Virtual Software Library. Copyright c/net, Inc.

SEARCH FOR PEOPLE

FINGER

Meta Information

URL:	http://www.cs.indiana.edu/finger/gateway
Resource Type:	World Wide Web site
Use:	finding e-mail addresses for individuals; finding additional information about individuals; checking who is currently logged into a particular server; primarily reference
Navigation:	search for e-mail addresses or domain names using "userid@domain-name" or "@domain-name" as the query syntax
Scope:	e-mail addresses; information about users
Volume:	all Internet accounts on servers that support the Finger protocol (some commercial, governmental, and military sites restrict Finger access to maintain privacy)
Searching Tips:	to find an individual, the query must be in the form of "userid@domain-name"; try the last name or a combination of first and last names as the userid; make an educated guess regarding the domain name; if you know the domain name, but can't find the userid, try fingering "@domain-name" to see a list of who's logged on; you might get lucky; if you have no luck, try Four11 or NetFind
Strengths:	great tool for finding additional information (e.g. phone numbers, home pages) about people when you already have their e-mail address
Weaknesses:	inflexible query syntax; not very useful for finding e-mail addresses unless you've already got most of the information
Updates:	daily
Questions:	Marc VanHeyningen, mvanheyn@cs.indiana.edu
Submissions:	n/a

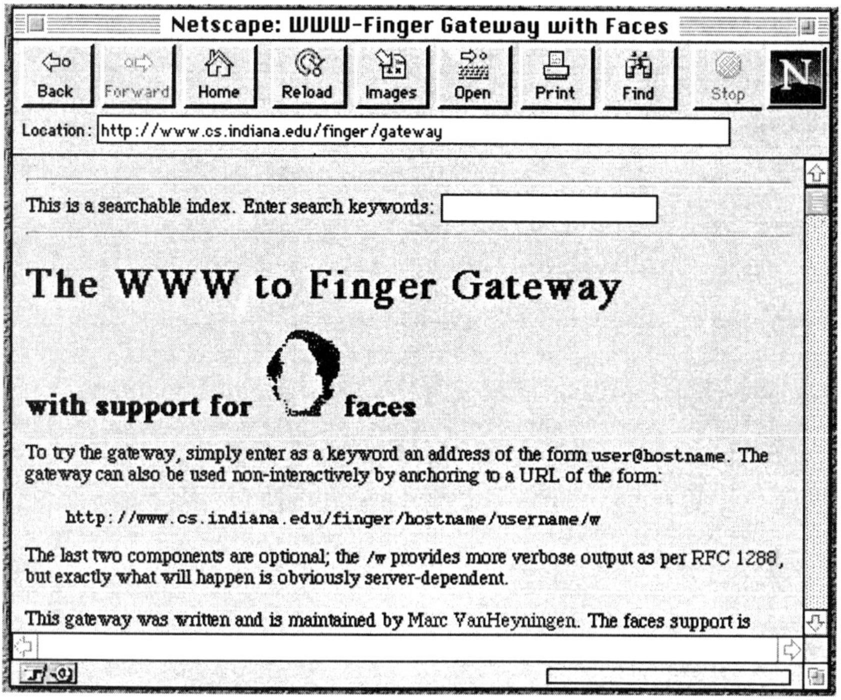

```
╔═══════════════════════════════════════════════════════════════════╗
║        Netscape: WWW-Finger Gateway with Faces                     ║
╠═══════════════════════════════════════════════════════════════════╣
║  ⟨⊐o    o⟩⊐    ⟨⌂⟩    ⟨◉⟩    ⟨▦⟩    ⇨o    ⟨▤⟩    ⟨▥⟩    ⟨◉⟩    ⟨N⟩   ║
║  Back  Forward  Home  Reload  Images  Open  Print  Find   Stop      ║
╠═══════════════════════════════════════════════════════════════════╣
║  Location: │http://www.cs.indiana.edu/finger/gateway            │   ║
╠═══════════════════════════════════════════════════════════════════╣
```

This is a searchable index. Enter search keywords: [   ]

The WWW to Finger Gateway

with support for ◯ faces

To try the gateway, simply enter as a keyword an address of the form `user@hostname`. The gateway can also be used non-interactively by anchoring to a URL of the form:

        `http://www.cs.indiana.edu/finger/hostname/username/w`

The last two components are optional; the /w provides more verbose output as per RFC 1288, but exactly what will happen is obviously server-dependent.

This gateway was written and is maintained by Marc VanHeyningen. The faces support is

Figure 7–34   Finger

Description

Finger is a tool which allows you to query remote servers for information about users on those servers. When looking for a user's e-mail address, you must enter a good guess according to the following syntax: userid@domain-name. The userid is typically some combination of the person's first and last name. A successful query will return the valid e-mail address(es) for that individual. You may also enter a valid e-mail address to find additional information about an individual such as a phone number or snail mail address or even whether they are currently logged in. Finally, you can enter a query in the form "@domain-name" (e.g. @sils.umich.edu) to see who is currently logged into that server. An important note to keep in mind when using Finger is that each system on the Internet can be configured to interact differently with your query. Some will simply refuse to allow your search. Additionally, users can often choose how much information about themselves to make available.

Evaluation

Finger is an excellent tool for finding additional information about an individual when you already know his or her e-mail address. It can also be very useful for determining who is currently logged into a server. Finger is not so useful for finding an e-mail address of an individual since you need to have so much information before you begin your search.

Sample Search

Objective: Heidi wants to find the phone number of her former professor, Joe Janes, at the University of Michigan's School of Information and Library Studies.

Heidi begins by entering "janes@umich.edu" as her query. Joe's last name is a good place to start as the userid and Heidi remembers the correct domain name. If she hadn't remembered, some guessing would have been necessary. The results show two exact matches for her query, one of which is "Joseph W. Janes" so Heidi tries "joseph.w.janes@umich.edu" as her query. This time the results show a business phone number and a valid e-mail address for Joe.

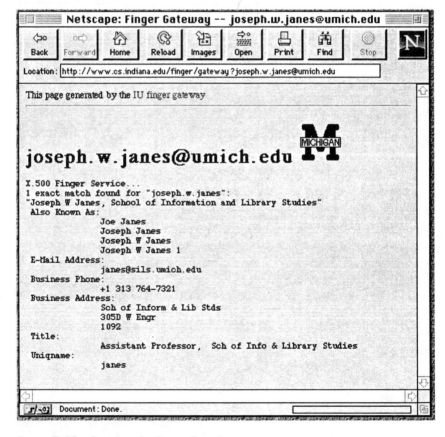

Figure 7–35   Results of a Finger Search

FOUR11 WHITE PAGES

Meta Information

URL:	http://www.four11.com/
Resource Type:	World Wide Web site
Use:	finding e-mail addresses and URLs of individuals; a reference tool
Navigation:	search for individuals by name, geographical location, and organizational affiliation
Scope:	a white page directory with contact information for individuals
Volume:	over one million individuals are listed
Searching Tips:	if you know the first and last name of the individual you are looking for, enter both; as a non-paying user you are restricted to a maximum of 30 hits, so you must be fairly specific; searching by current organization or past college or university can be helpful if you're not sure of the spelling of the individual's name
Strengths:	one of the fastest, most comprehensive, and user friendly tools for finding the e-mail addresses and URLs of individuals on the Internet; a flexible query interface and a fast search engine
Weaknesses:	the search limits placed on non-paying users can be frustrating; many Internet users are not listed in this directory
Updates:	daily
Questions:	comments@Four11.com
Submissions:	http://www.four11.com/cgi-bin/SledPython?Mq AddForm

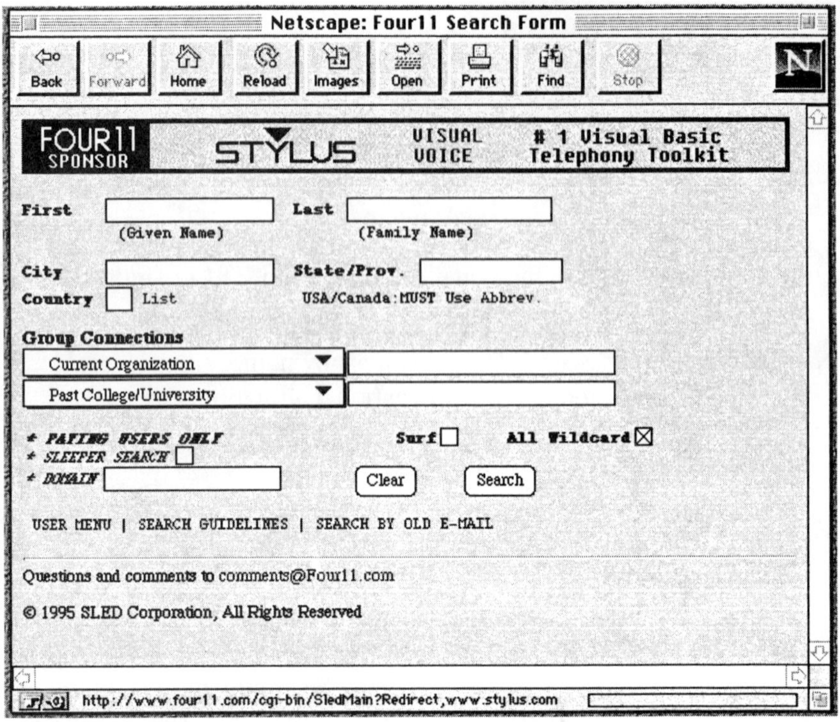

Figure 7–36   Four11 White Pages

Description

Four11 is an on-line white pages directory with contact information for over a million individuals. Users must register but no fee is currently required. Users may search Four11 using a combination of the individual's first name, last name, city, country, state, and group connections (e.g. organization, university, etc.). Results are displayed as a list of hits with first names, last names, and e-mail addresses. Valid e-mail addresses are displayed using "mailto" tags, so e-mail messages may be sent directly via the Web interface.

Evaluation

Four11 is one of the best tools for finding the Internet e-mail addresses of individuals. The query interface provides flexibility, the search engine is fast, and the database is large relative to other Internet white page directories. However, the database includes less than ten percent of all Internet users, so the odds of finding the person you are looking for are relatively slim. Overall, Four11 is a good place to start when looking for an e-mail address, but be prepared to use the phone.

Sample Search

Objective: Susan wants to find the e-mail address for Peter Morville, one of the authors of this book.

Having already registered to use Four11, Susan enters "peter" as the first name and "morville" as the last name. Two successful matches are displayed. The second provides three valid e-mail addresses and a link to Peter's personal web page.

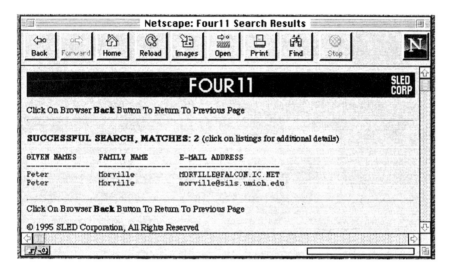

Figure 7–37   Results of a Sample Four11 Search

NETFIND

Meta Information

URL:	gopher://ds.internic.net:4320/1netfind
Resource Type:	Gopher site
Use:	finding e-mail addresses of individuals
Navigation:	search using three keys; the first key consists of a user's first or last name; the second and third are keywords pulled from their organization's name or location or the domain name of the server on which they have an account
Scope:	e-mail addresses of individuals
Volume:	all individuals who have e-mail accounts on servers that are configured to accept queries
Searching Tips:	use the individual's last name followed by a combination of organization's name, location, or domain name; when selecting a domain name from the list of matches, choose either a departmental server that looks promising (e.g. engin.umich.edu for the engineering department) or the broadest domain (e.g. umich.edu for the University of Michigan)
Strengths:	slightly more useful than Finger for finding individuals
Weaknesses:	confusing query interface; relatively low chance of success
Updates:	daily
Questions:	admin@ds.internic.net
Submissions:	n/a

Description

NetFind is a tool for finding the e-mail addresses of individuals. Queries must be entered in a "name key key" format (e.g. clinton white washington). The keys can be any combination of the organization's name, location, or domain name. After a query has been submitted, NetFind will return a list of domain names that match the two keys. The user must select a domain from that list. NetFind will then present a list of hits with the e-mail addresses of appropriate individuals.

Evaluation

If you know the name and organizational affiliation of an individual, NetFind can be helpful in finding their e-mail address. However, the query interface is quite unfriendly and inflexible and the chance of success is relatively low. NetFind is sometimes useful but be prepared to use the phone.

Sample Search

Objective: Jenny wants to find the e-mail address of Susan Wickhorst, a librarian at Bradley University in Peoria, Illinois.

Jenny begins by entering "Wickhorst" as the name and "Bradley Peoria" as the two keys. NetFind returns a list of several matching domain names which include "library.bradley.edu" and "bradley.edu". Jenny first tries the specific library domain with no luck. She then tries the more general Bradley domain and is rewarded with Susan's e-mail address.

WHOIS (MIT GATEWAY)

Meta Information

URL:	gopher://sipb.mit.edu/1B%3aInternet%20whois-%20servers
Resource Type:	Gopher site
Use:	finding contact information (phone numbers, e-mail addresses) for individuals; reference
Navigation:	search the Whois directories at a number of organizations by the individual's name
Scope:	contact information for individuals indexed in Whois directories
Volume:	roughly 70,000 individuals at over 150 organizations
Searching Tips:	use the keyword search capability of your Web browser to find the correct organization; begin with the individual's last name; if more than one hit is returned, refine your search using the individual's first name
Strengths:	fast simple searching for individuals
Weaknesses:	relatively small database; inability to search across organizations
Updates:	daily
Questions:	bug-whois@sipb.mit.edu (problems only)
Submissions:	Matt Power, mhpower@athena.mit.edu

Description

The Whois Gateway serves as a tool for finding the e-mail addresses and phone numbers of individuals. In order to search Whois, you need to select the organization with which the individual is affiliated from a list of roughly 150 organizations. Having selected the organization, you may search using the individual's last and/or first name. Whois will return a list of individuals who match your query. It may be necessary to refine the query, since Whois will only display the contact information once the

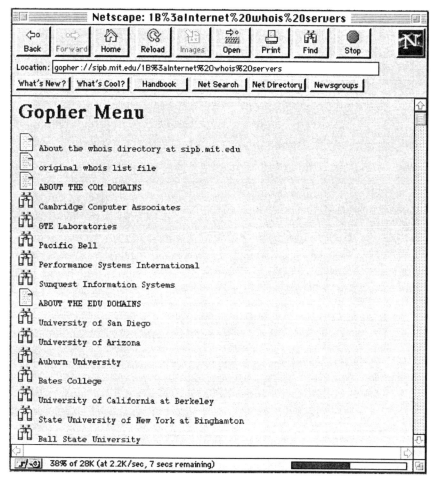

Figure 7–38   The Whois Gateway

number of matches has been reduced to one. The contact information may include an e-mail address, phone number, department, and postal address.

Evaluation

If you know the organizational affiliation of the individual you are looking for, and that organization happens to be included in the Whois listing, then Whois provides a fast and relatively straightforward means of accessing contact information. However, the database is rather small and you may not always know the organizational affiliation. The inability to search across organizations and the rather primitive interface add to the problems of Whois. Finally, the information provided about individuals varies from organization to organization. In summary, Whois can sometimes be helpful, but be prepared to use other Internet search tools or to pick up the telephone.

Sample Search

Objective: Malcolm wants to find the e-mail address for David Gifford, a professor at the Massachusetts Institute of Technology (MIT).

Malcolm first uses the keyword search capability of his Web browser to find organizations with "institute" in their name. After a few tries, he finds and selects MIT. He then enters "Gifford" as his keyword. Whois returns three matches, one of which is "David Gifford" and prompts Malcolm to refine his search. Malcolm then searches on "Gifford David" and is rewarded with his contact information which includes a phone number and e-mail address.

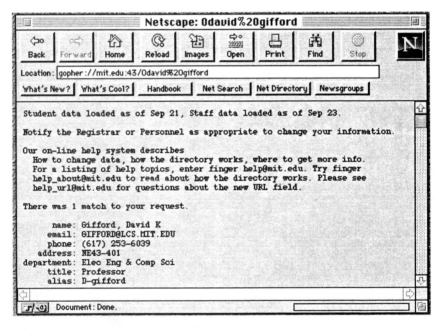

Figure 7–39   Results of a Sample Whois Search

X.500 GATEWAY

Meta Information

URL: gopher://judgmentday.rs.itd.umich.edu:7777/1

Resource Type: Gopher site

Use: finding contact information (phone numbers, e-mail addresses) for individuals

Navigation: select the appropriate geographical location and organization; search using a combination of the individual's first and last name

Scope: contact information for individuals at select organizations

Volume: over 300 organizations

Searching Tips: use the keyword searching capability of your Web browser to find the appropriate location and organization; begin with the individual's last name; if necessary, refine the search by using first and last name

Strengths: relatively straightforward browsing and query interfaces

Weaknesses: limited database; inability to search across organizations

Updates: daily

Questions: x500@umich.edu

Submissions: n/a

Description

The X.500 Gateway provides users with the ability to search for the contact information of individuals. Users must first browse through a listing of geographic locations and select the appropriate country or state. Users must then browse through a list of organizations and select the correct one. Finally, users may search for an individual using a combination of first and last name as the keyword(s). Displayed results may include phone and fax numbers, e-mail addresses, and snail mail addresses.

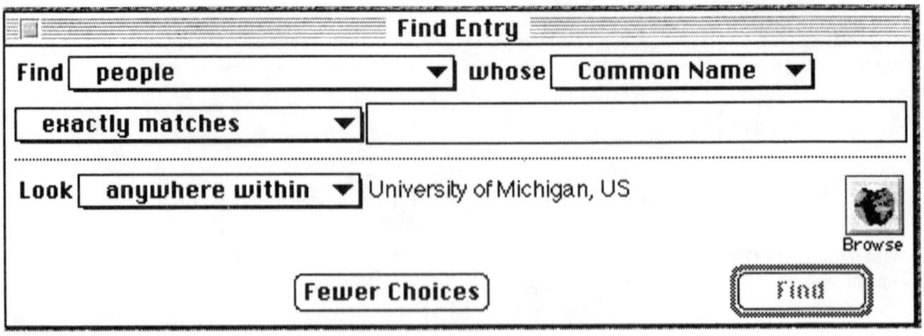

Figure 7–40   The X.500 Directory Service

Evaluation

If you know the organizational affiliation of the individual you are looking for, and that organization happens to be included in the X.500 listing,
then X.500 provides a fast and relatively straightforward means of accessing contact information. However, the database is far from comprehensive and you may not always know the organizational affiliation. The inability to search across organizations and the rather primitive interface
add to the problems of the X.500 Gateway. In short, X.500 can be a useful tool for finding contact information, but be prepared to try the other
Internet search tools or to pick up the telephone.

Sample Search

Objective: Tony wants to find the e-mail address of Michael Cohen,
                  a professor at the University of Michigan.

Tony begins by selecting "USA" as the country and then uses the keyword capability of his Web browser to find the "University of Michigan."
He then enters "cohen" as his keyword. Tony is presented with an alphabetically ordered list of matches. He browses down the list until he finds
the correct Michael Cohen entry.

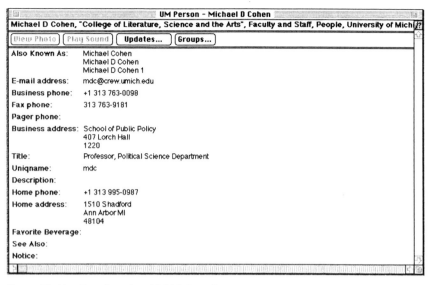

Figure 7–41   Results of an X.500 Search

SEARCH FOR COMMUNITIES OF PEOPLE

DARTMOUTH'S LIST OF LISTS

Meta Information

URL:	http://alpha.acast.nova.edu/cgi-bin/lists
Resource Type:	World Wide Web site
Use:	finding electronic mail discussion groups
Navigation:	keyword search a database of Bitnet and Internet interest groups which includes titles, addresses, and in many cases descriptions of the discussion groups
Scope:	electronic mail discussion groups
Volume:	over 5,900 groups
Searching Tips:	begin with a relatively specific keyword; if no hits are returned, try a more general keyword and/or try a keyword stem (e.g. for philosophy try phil); to effect a Boolean search, use one keyword in your initial query, and then apply the second keyword to the resulting set of hits using your Web browser's search capability
Strengths:	a relatively large and content-rich database; a fast search engine
Weaknesses:	a fairly inflexible query interface
Updates:	weekly
Questions:	n/a
Submissions:	n/a

Description

The Dartmouth List is a tool for finding electronic mail discussion groups on a particular topic. Users may keyword search a database which provides titles, addresses, and descriptions of each discussion group. Users are presented with a list of matching entries with the meta information for each group.

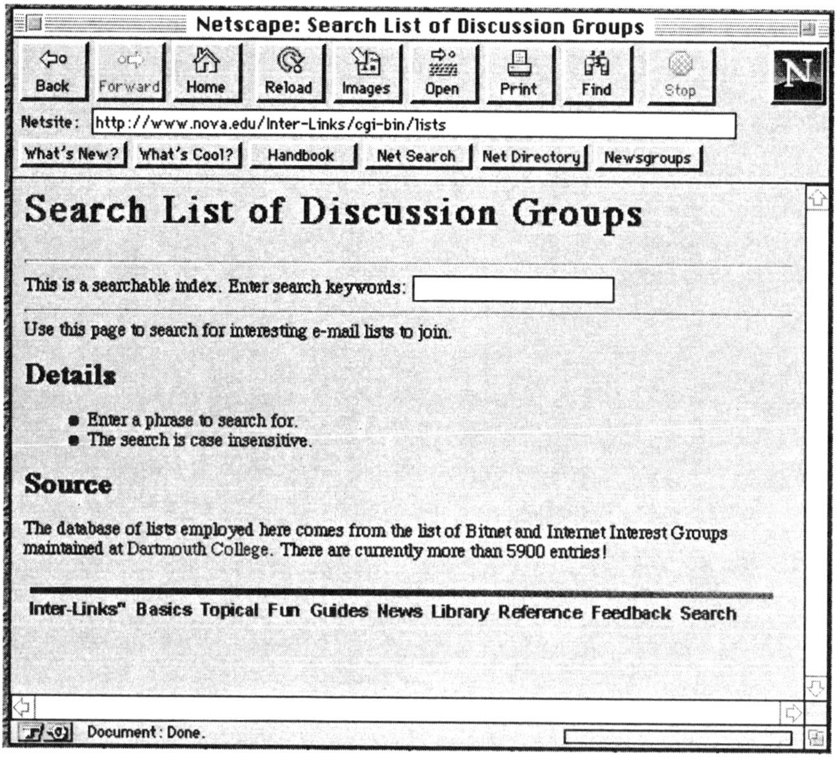

Figure 7–42   Dartmouth's List of Lists

Evaluation

The Dartmouth List provides access to one of the richer and more comprehensive databases of electronic mail discussion groups. The search engine is very fast and the information is presented in a nicely formatted manner. On the down side, the query interface is rather basic and inflexible. Boolean search capabilities are not provided. Overall, the Dartmouth List is a useful tool for finding electronic mail discussion groups.

Sample Search

Objective: Bob is looking for a discussion group on the topic of fishing.

Bob enters "fishing" as his keyword and is rewarded by a listing of one mailing list. He tries again using "fish" as the keyword. About 20 matching lists are displayed, some useful and some not so useful.

DEJANEWS

Meta Information

URL:	http://www.dejanews.com/dnhome.html
Resource Type:	World Wide Web site
Use:	searching through archived Usenet newsgroup postings; finding information, people, and communities of people; primarily useful for research
Navigation:	keyword search of the full text of Usenet postings; Boolean (AND, OR, NOT) capabilities; limit by currency of information; limit number of hits to be displayed
Scope:	very broad; most newsgroups are indexed; past month of postings
Volume:	four gigabytes of data; thousands of newsgroups; hundreds of thousands of postings
Searching Tips:	given the large volume and heterogeneity of the database, very specific searches are most profitable; make good use of the "&" capability; read the "how to use Boolean connectors" section under "help" for more details
Strengths:	a huge database and a fast search engine; ability to use Boolean operators makes searching much more efficient
Weaknesses:	variable size, content, and quality of postings; display of results not formatted nicely
Updates:	weekly
Questions:	comment@dejanews.com, help@dejanews.com
Submissions:	n/a

Description

DejaNews allows users to search the full text of an extensive archive of Usenet newsgroup postings. The most recent month's postings are available. Thousands of newsgroups are covered. Users may employ nested

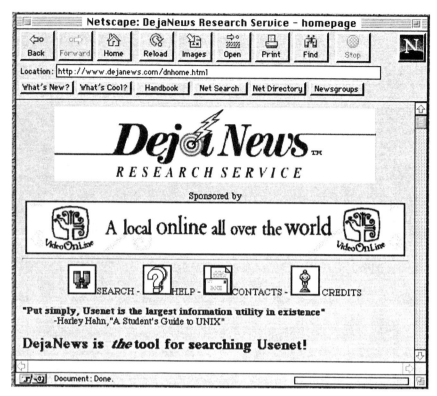

Figure 7–43   DejaNews

Boolean queries and wildcards. Results are presented as a list of messages. For each message, the date of posting, subject line, newsgroup, and author is listed. Selecting the subject line leads the user to the full text of the posting.

Evaluation

The extensive database combined with the flexible searching capabilities and fast search engine makes DejaNews an excellent tool for searching through Usenet postings. If you're interested in what people are saying about a particular topic or want to find a few good newsgroups to subscribe to, DejaNews is the right tool to use. On the down side, Usenet postings vary widely in terms of quality, length, and intended audience. Many of the postings are not worth reading. This makes the process of browsing for useful information a tedious one. Overall, this is a great tool if you need to search through Usenet postings.

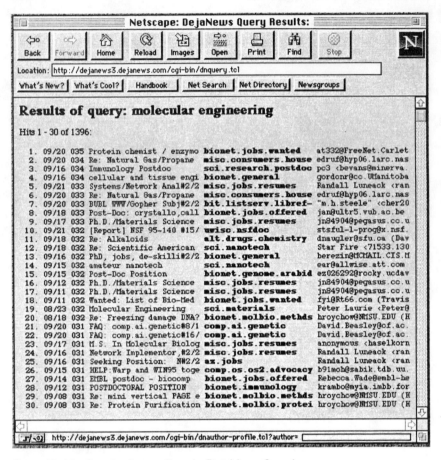

Figure 7–44   Results from a Sample DejaNews Search

Sample Search

Objective: Garth wants to know if there are any newsgroups where people are discussing molecular engineering.

Garth enters "molecular & engineering" as his keywords. He is rewarded by a long list of hits consisting of the date, a hyperlinked subject line, the name of the newsgroup, and the author's e-mail address for each message.

FAQ ARCHIVE

Meta Information

URL:	http://www.cs.ruu.nl/cgi-bin/faqwais
Resource Type:	World Wide Web site
Use:	search through FAQs (frequently asked questions) and other informative postings to the news.answers Usenet group; finding Usenet groups; finding information; primarily a research tool
Navigation:	browse by archive name and subject; browse by newsgroup; search the full text of the archive by keyword
Scope:	broad; FAQs and articles posted in news.answers Usenet group
Volume:	over 600 postings
Searching Tips:	keyword searching is definitely the place to start; try a fairly specific keyword or two; if no hits are returned, try a related term; note that if you browse by archive name and subject or newsgroup, you can use the keyword searching feature of your Web browser
Strengths:	a great way to find Usenet newsgroups on a particular topic
Weaknesses:	lack of Boolean search capability
Updates:	daily
Questions:	www@cs.ruu.nl
Submissions:	n/a

Description

The FAQ Archive provides a means of searching the FAQs and related postings to the news.answers Usenet newsgroup. These FAQs contain background information about each newsgroup and the topics covered by that newsgroup. Users may browse through a list of the newsgroup

Figure 7–45   The FAQ Archive

names and subjects or may keyword search the full text of the archive. Multiple keywords may be entered separated by spaces. Results are presented as a ranked list of FAQs and articles. The subject of each FAQ or article serves as a hyperlink to the full text. Cross references to other newsgroups within each article are also hyperlinked.

Evaluation

The FAQ Archive is an excellent tool for identifying potentially useful newsgroups on a particular topic. The content of FAQs is typically indicative of the subject matter of a given newsgroup. Not only does searching the FAQ Archive help the user to identify useful newsgroups, but it also provides important background information about those newsgroups. The keyword search feature is simple and fast. On the down side, since FAQs tend to be rather verbose and it's not possible to make use of Boolean operators, searches tend to produce a substantial number of false drops. It's often necessary to browse through a long list of hits to find a few useful newsgroups. Overall, if you're looking for some relevant newsgroups, the FAQ Archive is a good tool to use.

Sample Search

Objective: Beth wants to find a newsgroup in which people are discussing artificial life.

Beth begins her search by using "artificial life" as her keywords. She then browses through the result list and selects "ai-faq alife," a promising subject line. The introduction confirms that this is a relevant newsgroup and also supplies hyperlinks to a couple of related newsgroups.

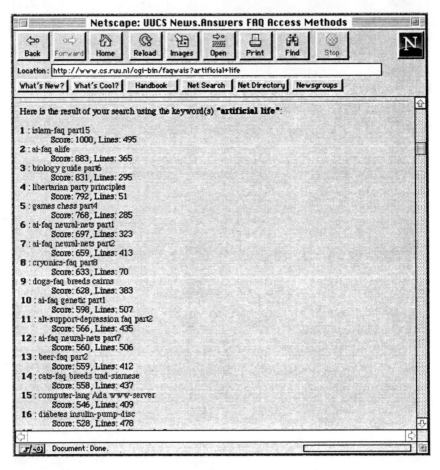

Figure 7–46   Results of a Sample FAQ Archive Search

FUZZY FAQ

Meta Information

URL:	http://www.nexial.nl/cgi-bin/faq
Resource Type:	World Wide Web site
Use:	searching FAQs of Usenet newsgroups; finding newsgroups; finding information; primarily a research tool
Navigation:	fuzzy search the full text of FAQs using keywords; modify number of hits to be displayed and level of fuzziness to be accepted
Scope:	broad; newsgroup FAQs
Volume:	more than 4,000 FAQs; 100 Megabytes of data
Searching Tips:	restrict to minimal fuzziness; use a couple of fairly specific keywords
Strengths:	a very large database of FAQs
Weaknesses:	the fuzziness of the search feature produces large numbers of false drops
Updates:	daily
Questions:	info@nexial.nl
Submissions:	n/a

Description

Fuzzy FAQ is a tool for searching through a database of FAQs for Usenet newsgroups. Users may enter one or more keywords, limit the number of hits to be displayed, and adjust the level of fuzziness to be accepted. Fuzziness refers to the degree to which a word in the database must match the keyword. For instance, if a user enters "pumpkins" as a keyword, a search with minimal fuzziness might only return "pumpkins" and "pumpkin" while a very fuzzy search would return everything from "pumpkin" to "pugilist." Results are presented as a ranked list of hyperlinked subject lines followed by message excerpts with keyword in context. Selecting the subject line of a message will take you to the full text.

Figure 7–47   Fuzzy FAQ

Evaluation

The large database provides for more comprehensive searching of Usenet newsgroup FAQs than is available with other tools. The interface is designed fairly well and the search engine is fast. The keyword in the context display feature is a nice touch. However, the use of fuzzy search technology on such a large and heterogeneous database does not seem well advised. Use of any but the most minimal fuzziness settings seems to result in large numbers of false drops. Overall, a useful tool for finding Usenet FAQs with an unusual and somewhat frustrating searching algorithm.

Sample Search

Objective: Charles is looking for a newsgroup or two on the topic of gothic art.

Charles uses "gothic art" as his keywords. Before beginning the search, he reduces the level of fuzziness to "minimal" and the total number of hits to "30." The results are displayed as a ranked list of hyperlinked subject lines followed by keywords in context.

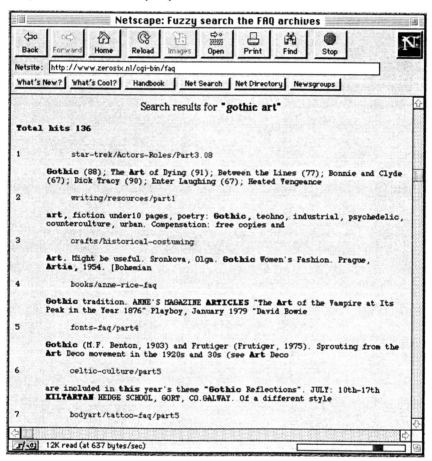

Figure 7–48   Results of a Sample Search Using Fuzzy FAQ

MAILBASE

Meta Information

URL:	http://mailbase.ac.uk/
Resource Type:	World Wide Web site
Use:	finding electronic mail discussion groups on a particular topic; reference
Navigation:	browse alphabetical title listing; search a database of discussion group descriptions using keywords
Scope:	electronic mail discussion groups originating in the United Kingdom
Volume:	over 700 discussion groups
Searching Tips:	the keyword search tool is far more useful than the alphabetical listings; start with one keyword, but if you need to refine your query, take advantage of the Boolean capabilities
Strengths:	a simple yet flexible query interface with support for Boolean operators and the use of wildcards for truncation
Weaknesses:	poor organization of the main page; you need to scroll down several screens to find the searching facilities; limited database
Updates:	monthly
Questions:	mailbase-helpline@mailbase.ac.uk
Submissions:	n/a

Description

Mailbase is a tool for finding electronic mail discussion groups on a particular topic. Mailbase and the discussion groups it provides access to originate in the United Kingdom, so there's a strong emphasis towards topics of British interest. Users may browse through an alphabetical listing of discussion group titles or keyword search a database of descriptions. For each matching group, Mailbase provides a description of that group and a list of members with their e-mail addresses. Additionally, users may browse or search the archives of that discussion group.

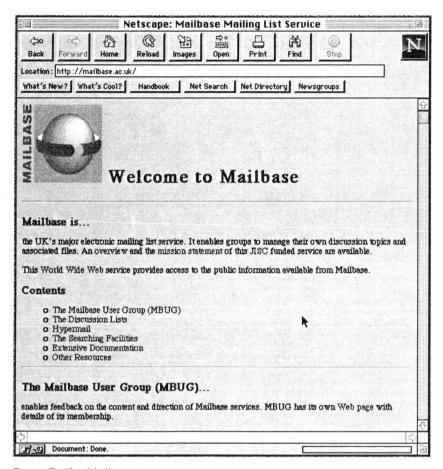

Figure 7–49   Mailbase

Evaluation

The query interface is well designed and the extensive information provided for each discussion group makes Mailbase a very nice tool to use. The main page is rather poorly laid out, but that doesn't present a major problem. The primary limitation of Mailbase is the relatively small database of discussion groups. However, if you're looking for discussion groups on topics of interest to the British, this is a great place to look.

Sample Search

Objective: Sam would like to find a discussion group on the topic of politics in China.

Sam begins his search by entering "politic° and Chin°" as his query. Mailbase returns a couple of matches. Sam chooses one and Mailbase displays a menu which provides Sam with access to a description of the discussion group, a list of group members and their e-mail addresses, and contact information for the list moderator. Sam may also browse or search through the archives of the group.

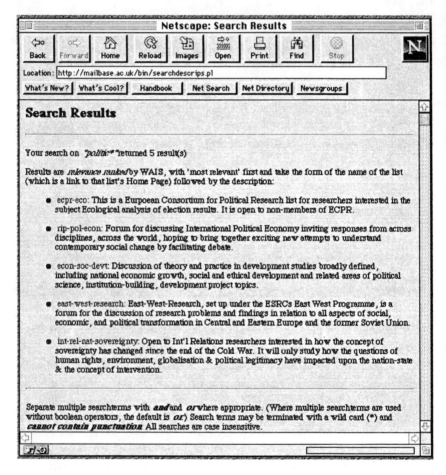

Figure 7–50   Results of a Mailbase Search

PUBLICLY ACCESSIBLE MAILING LISTS (PAML)

Meta Information

URL:	http://www.NeoSoft.com:80/internet/paml/
Resource Type:	World Wide Web site
Use:	finding electronic mail discussion groups
Navigation:	browse topical index or alphabetical name index
Scope:	electronic mail discussion groups on more than 150 topics
Volume:	over 1,350 mailing lists
Searching Tips:	use the subject index to identify mailing lists within broad categories; for a very specific search, bring up the alphabetical name index and try some keyword searches using your Web browser's keyword search capability
Strengths:	the subject index provides a fast easy way to find a few interesting groups
Weaknesses:	the complete contents of each index are on one Web page which leads to painfully slow loading of those pages; no built in keyword search capability
Updates:	monthly
Questions:	Stephanie da Silva, arielle@taronga.com
Submissions:	Stephanie da Silva, arielle@taronga.com

Description

Publicly Accessible Mailing Lists (PAML) is a tool for finding electronic mailing lists on a particular topic. PAML may be searched using a topical index or an alphabetical name index. For each mailing list, PAML provides the title, contact person, purpose, subscription information, and keywords.

Evaluation

For finding a few electronic discussion groups on a particular topic, the subject index of PAML serves as a fairly useful tool. The database is relatively current and the information presented in a nice format. The major problem lies in the fact that the complete contents of each index appear

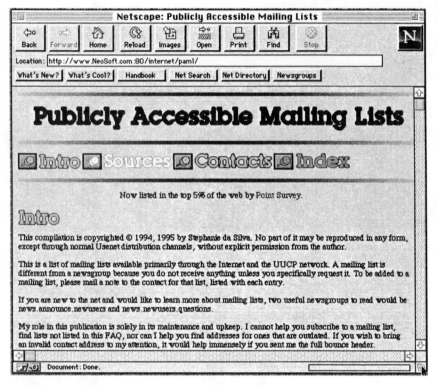

Figure 7–51   Publicly Accessible Mailing Lists (PAML)

on one Web page. This forces the user to wait for the entire page to load
before being able to really use the index. Some redesign could make the
user's experience much less frustrating. Overall, PAML is a useful tool
for finding electronic discussion groups.

Sample Search

Objective: Becky has heard that there is an environmental discus-
                    sion group sponsored by the Sierra Club and would like
                    to find and join it.

Becky selects the subject index and waits for the page to load completely.
She then browses through the index and selects the "environment" category. Within that category she finds several mailing lists, one of which is
called the "Sierra Club."

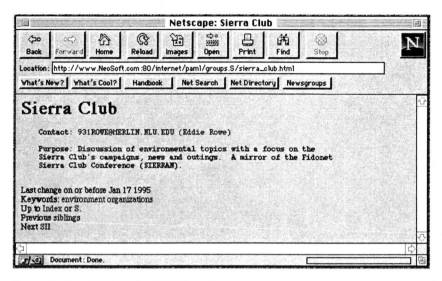

Figure 7–52   Results of a PAML Search

SCHOLARLY E-CONFERENCES

Meta Information

URL:	http://www.mid.net/KOVACS/
Resource Type:	World Wide Web site
Use:	finding electronic mailing lists and newsgroups
Navigation:	browse by topic or search a database of abstracts using keywords
Scope:	electronic mailing lists and newsgroups of a scholarly nature
Volume:	over 1,790 conferences in 62 different categories
Searching Tips:	for a quick and dirty search, try entering a keyword via the query interface; for a more extensive search, try a combination of browsing and searching; note that two words separated by a space are interpreted as a phrase (i.e. "computer technology" will only return records with that exact phrase). Boolean searching is not provided for.
Strengths:	a rich and well formatted database; the combination of browsing and searching provides added flexibility
Weaknesses:	database limited to conferences of a scholarly nature
Updates:	monthly
Questions:	Diane Kovacs, di@kovacs.com
Submissions:	Diane Kovacs, di@kovacs.com

Description

The Directory of Scholarly E-conferences is a database of electronic mailing lists and Usenet newsgroups that are of a scholarly nature. Each record provides the list name, title, subscription address, moderator's e-mail address, and keywords. Users may browse through a subject-oriented hierarchy or search the full text of the records using keyword queries. A keyword search will return a hit list of hyperlinked titles of conferences. Users may select each title in turn to view the conference description.

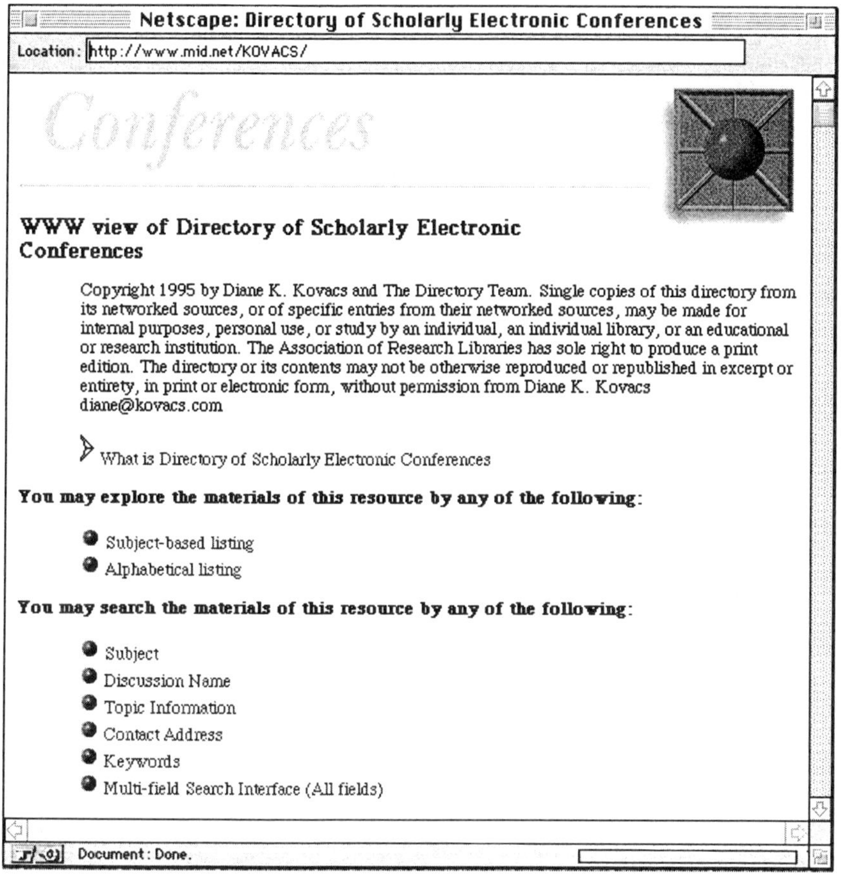

Figure 7–53   The Directory of Scholarly E-conferences

Evaluation

For locating academically oriented on-line discussion groups, the Directory of Scholarly E-conferences is one of the best tools available. The database is fairly extensive, well managed, and current. By selecting only conferences of a scholarly nature, it filters out many of the less interesting mailing lists and newsgroups. The browsing capability provides a nice way to develop a sense of the scope and breadth of the collection. The keyword search capability provides a quick way to find potentially useful groups. The lack of a Boolean search capability is unfortunate but doesn't present a large problem given the size of the database. Overall, if you're looking for academically oriented discussion groups, this is a great place to start.

Sample Search

Objective: George would like to find some on-line discussion groups
               that are focused around the topic of geology.

George begins by browsing the topical categories. He uses the keyword
searching capability of his Web browser to identify the geology category
where he finds a listing of several relevant discussion lists. He then tries
using the keyword search capability and enters "geology" as his query
term. He is rewarded with a list of several discussion lists, some of which
were not located in the geology category.

Appendix I

Quick Index to Internet Searching Tools and Resources

Note: An online collection of pointers to all the tools and resources covered in this book is available in the **Internet Searching Center** at *http://www.lib.umich.edu/chouse/searching/find.html*

VIRTUAL LIBRARIES

Clearinghouse for Subject-Oriented Internet Resource Guides
http://www.lib.umich.edu/chouse/chhome.html
Internet Public Library
http://ipl.org/
Magellan Internet Directory
http://mckinley.mckinley.com/
Planet Earth Virtual Library
http://www.nosc.mil/planet_earth/info.html
Special Internet Connections (The Yanoff List)
http://www.uwm.edu/Mirror/inet.services.html
Whole Internet Catalog
http://www.gnn.com/gnn/wic/index.html
World Wide Web Virtual Library
http://www.w3.org/hypertext/DataSources/bySubject/Overview.html

INTERNET DIRECTORIES

BizWeb
http://www.bizweb.com/
Open Market's Commercial Sites Index
http://www.directory.net/
TradeWave Galaxy
http://www.einet.net/galaxy.html
World Wide Yellow Pages
http://www.yellow.com/
Yahoo
http://www.yahoo.com/

SEARCH TOOLS

Search for Information

ALIWEB
http://web.nexor.co.uk/public/aliweb/aliweb.html
CUI W3 Catalog
http://cuiwww.unige.ch/cgi-bin/w3catalog
Domain Name Search Tool
http://ibc.wustl.edu/domain_form.html
Harvest
http://www.town.hall.org/brokers/www-home-pages/query.html
InfoSeek ($)
http://www.infoseek.com:80/Home
JumpStation II
http://js.stir.ac.uk/jsbin/jsii
Lycos
http://www.lycos.com/
NlightN
http://www.nlightn.com/
Open Text Web Index
http://www.opentext.com:8080/omw.html
Point
http://www.pointcom.com/
Veronica Gateway
http://www.scs.unr.edu/veronica.html
WAIS Gateway
http://www.wais.com/directory-of-servers.html

Wandex
http://www.netgen.com/cgi/wandex
WebCrawler
http://webcrawler.com/
W3 Worm
http://www.cs.colorado.edu/home/mcbryan/WWWW.html

Search for Software

Archie Directory
http://pubweb.nexor.co.uk/public/archie/servers.html
ArchiePlex (CUI implementation)
http://cuiwww.unige.ch/./archieplexform.html
ArchiePlex (NASA implementation)
http://www.lerc.nasa.gov/Doc/archieplex.html
ArchiePlex (NCSA implementation)
http://hoohoo.ncsa.uiuc.edu/archie.html
Virtual Software Library
http://vsl.cnet.com/

Search for People

Finger
http://www.cs.indiana.edu/finger/gateway
Four11 White Pages
http://www.four11.com/
NetFind
gopher://ds.internic.net:4320/1netfind
Whois (MIT Gateway)
gopher://sipb.mit.edu/1B%3aInternet%20whois%20servers
X.500
gopher://judgmentday.rs.itd.umich.edu:7777/1

Search for Communities of People

Dartmouth's List of Lists
http://alpha.acast.nova.edu/cgi-bin/lists
DejaNews
http://www.dejanews.com/dnhome.html
FAQ Archive
http://www.cs.ruu.nl/cgi-bin/faqwais
Fuzzy FAQ
http://www.nexial.nl/cgi-bin/faq

Mailbase
http://mailbase.ac.uk/
Publicly Accessible Mailing Lists (PAML)
http://www.NeoSoft.com:80/internet/paml/
Scholarly E-conferences
http://www.mid.net/KOVACS/

Appendix II

Regular Expressions

Regular expressions come from the frontier days of the Internet when scientists, military researchers, and computer geeks ruled the Net—and the rest of us couldn't even figure out how to send e-mail. Those days have passed and the Internet is much friendlier, but unfortunately a few user-hostile remnants such as regular expressions still remain. The language of regular expressions provides syntactical rules for conducting advanced keyword searches. A number of Internet search tools provide the user with the ability to search using these expressions. If you've used the *grep* searching tool for UNIX, you may be familiar with this arcane language. If not, here's a brief primer to help you take advantage of some of the most useful regular expressions. For a more comprehensive listing, consult one of the many UNIX books.

PATTERN MATCHING WITH REGULAR EXPRESSIONS

.   single character wildcard (e.g. c.t will return "cat" and "cot")

*   multiple character wildcard (e.g. c*t will return "cat" and "cot" and "cataract" and so on) may be used at the beginning, middle, or end of a word or in place of a word

[]   a string enclosed in brackets matches any one character in the string (e.g. [mM]ichigan will return "michigan" and "Michigan")

^   a regular expression preceeded by a ^ will match only those
            lines that begin with the expression
            (e.g. '^Jackson' will return Jackson Pollack but not Michael
            Jackson)

$ a regular expression followed by a $ will match only those lines
            that end with the expression
            (e.g. 'She smiled at me$' would not return "She smiled at me
            yesterday")

Acknowledgments

This book stands as testament to the vast potential for communication, collaboration, and information sharing represented by the Internet. Without the thousands of documents, literary works, databases, images, and software programs made available for free by individuals, universities, and libraries around the world, there would be *no reason* to search the Internet. And without the topical guides, virtual libraries, directories, and search tools again made available for free, there would be *no way* to search the Internet. We take this opportunity to thank the thousands of volunteers who have helped to make the Internet such a rich and interesting place to work and play.

Peter: Thanks to Lou Rosenfeld and Joe Janes for nurturing my interests in information system design and on-line searching. You've taught me (almost) everything I know about the Internet. And thanks to Malcolm, Judith, Paul, Rosalind, and Susan for providing the guidance, patience, and support that allow me to reach my goals.

Lou: Thanks to Peter Morville for taking the lead in writing this book; it benefits information professionals and indeed all Internet searchers to learn about finding information from the librarian's perspective. I thank Joe Janes for his mentorship and for encouraging us and many others to take on such ambitious projects, despite our own self-doubts. And I thank my parents, who still aren't quite sure what their son does, but are thrilled nonetheless.

Joe thanks and acknowledges the students in his on-line searching classes over the past several years. Many of his ideas have emerged there and evolved over the years, so he appreciates the difficult questions and interesting ideas which have been tossed around.

We'd all like to thank Rich Wiggins, Sara Ryan, Stephanie Walker, Fred Zimmerman, and Tim Howes for contributing their unique perspectives to this book. And finally, we'd like to thank Patricia Glass Schuman and Charles Harmon at Neal-Schuman Publishers for recognizing the need for this book and helping to make it happen.

Glossary

Adjacency
An adjacency operator is used in online searching to specify the order and proximity of terms. For example, asking for LIVING (ADJ) WILL would only return documents in which the word LIVING is followed immediately by WILL.

AND
A Boolean operator used to identify the intersection of two or more terms. For example, asking for APPLES AND ORANGES would only return those documents in which both words occur.

Bookmark
Many World Wide Web browsers provide a feature that allows you to "bookmark" Web sites to which you would like to return. The resulting "hotlist" makes it easy to return to those sites at a later time.

Boolean searching
Boolean searching relies on the use of operators such as AND, OR, and NOT to form sophisticated queries (e.g. State AND Michigan NOT University).

Controlled vocabulary
A predetermined set of terms to be used in the labeling of document and menu titles. While controlled vocabularies have been used widely in traditional libraries, they do not work as well in the dynamic and chaotic environment of the Internet.

Domain names
All "hosts" or computers directly connected to the Internet are assigned a unique address or domain name. Examples include *sils.umich.edu* and *argus-inc.com*.

FAQ

Many electronic mailing lists and Usenet newsgroups provide a FAQ or list of frequently asked questions. FAQs are designed to help new members become familiar with a group and to reduce the burden on existing members to constantly answer the same basic questions.

Flame

A flame or hostile e-mail message may be sent privately via e-mail or publicly via a discussion group. Public flames may result in "flame wars" which involve dozens of angry messages posted in a public forum.

FTP

FTP or File Transfer Protocol is a tool for uploading and downloading files to and from Internet host computers. Hundreds of public domain software applications are freely available via anonymous FTP sites. Typing "anonymous" as your login at these sites allows you access to these public files.

Home page

A home page is the front page or main menu of a Web site. The term is also used to refer to an individual's personal Web page.

Hypertext

Documents on the World Wide Web are connected via hypertext links. These links can be words or images and can connect to words, images, video clips, or other documents. Hypertext allows for seamless navigation between different documents, media formats, and computers.

Internet directories

Internet directories or "collections of resources maintained by the global Internet community" are currently the most comprehensive, easy-to-use tools for finding Internet information.

Internet resource discovery

Internet resource discovery is an iterative and interactive process in which you employ virtual libraries, directories, search tools, and communities of people to find textual or hypermedia documents, software applications, and more.

Lurkers

People who observe the traffic on electronic mailing lists and Usenet newsgroups without contributing their own postings are called lurkers.

Meta information

Meta information is information *about* other information. For example, the meta information for an Internet resource might specify the URL, the author, and the date that resource was last updated.

Natural language query

A search engine such as WAIS that accepts natural language queries allows you to enter a query in the same manner that you might ask the question of a person. For example, my query might be as follows: *Show me all the documents you have about President Clinton's health care policy.*

Netiquette

Netiquette refers to the often unwritten rules of conduct in the Internet's online communities. These rules tend to vary from community to community.

NOT

A Boolean operator used to exclude documents with certain terms from the result set. For example, DOG NOT POODLE would return all documents with the term DOG except those that include the word POODLE.

OR

A Boolean operator used to identify the union of two or more terms. For example, ORANGES OR APPLES would return all documents that include either the word ORANGES or the word APPLES. Documents with both terms would also be included.

Precision

Precision refers to the relative number of "false drops" in the result set of a search. In a high precision search, most, if not all of the resulting hits should be relevant and useful.

Proximity

Proximity refers to the closeness but not the order of terms in a document. For example, you may wish to search for documents in which the terms ONLINE and SEARCHING appear within 3 words of each other. Such a search would return documents with the phrase ONLINE SEARCHING and SEARCHING IN THE ONLINE ENVIRONMENT.

Recall
Recall refers to the ratio of relevant documents retrieved to the set of all relevant documents. In a high recall search, most if not all of the relevant documents in the database (or on the Internet) are retrieved.

Reference
The goal of a reference or ad-hoc query is to find the answer to a specific question.

Relevance ranking
A number of search tools such as WAIS and Lycos employ algorithms that rank hits according to their judgement of relevance. These algorithms typically evaluate the number of times terms occur in the document, where they occur in the document, and how close to each other two or more terms occur.

Research
To conduct research is to search or investigate carefully. The goal of a research investigation is to find all or most of the information on a particular topic.

Substring
A portion of a string, starting at a certain character position, and proceeding for a certain number of characters. In a substring search, partial word matches are returned. For example, a substring search on the word LIBRARY might return LIBRARY, LIBRARIES, and LIBRARIANS.

Term weighting
When using a search engine that employs a relevance ranking algorithm, term weighting allows you to assign greater significance to one or more terms. For example, you might search for documents with the phrase HEALTH CARE, but assign more weight to the term HEALTH.

Thread
A thread is a specific topic of discussion within the broader range of topics discussed on an electronic mailing list or Usenet newsgroup.

Truncation
Truncation refers to the use of wildcards to search for variations on a particular word. For example, a search on UNIVERS° might return UNIVERSITY and UNIVERSE and UNIVERSAL.

URL
Each resource on the World Wide Web has a unique address known as a URL or Uniform Resource Locator. Users can access these resources by entering their URLs into a Web browser. (e.g. http://www.umich.edu/)

Virtual libraries
Virtual libraries or "value added collections of Internet resources" provide a taste of the value that librarians can add to the Internet through the application of traditional skills in a vastly non-traditional environment. Through the identification, selection, organization, description, and evaluation of Internet information resources, librarians create virtual libraries which help people to find information, software, and communities of people.

White pages
White page directories such as Four11 and X.500 provide access to contact information for individuals.

Yellow pages
Yellow page directories such as Open Market's Directory of Commercial Services and the World Wide Yellow Pages provide access to information about companies and their products and services.

Index*

---

*Numbers in bold indicate illustrations.

About the Authors

Peter Morville is vice president of Argus Associates and managing editor of the Clearinghouse for Subject-Oriented Internet Resource Guides. Argus specializes in the design of large-scale information systems and places emphasis on information organization and indexing, information resource development, presentation, and ease of use. Morville has a master's degree in Information and Library Studies from the University of Michigan and has written subject specific Internet Resource Guides on such diverse topics as philosophy and nanotechnology. Published articles include *The Internet as Research Tool* (The Net, July 1995) and *Building Subject Specific Guides to Internet Resources* (Journal of Collection Building, Fall 1995). A personal home page is available at *http://argus-inc.com/morville.html*.

Louis Rosenfeld is president of Argus Associates and director of the Clearinghouse for Subject-Oriented Internet Resource Guides. Mr. Rosenfeld is lead editor of a series of Internet reference volumes entitled *The Internet Compendium* (Neal-Schuman, 1995). He has worked as an instructor and librarian at the University of Michigan, and has given presentations on networked information services in North America and Europe.

Joseph Janes is an assistant professor in the School of Information and Library Studies at the University of Michigan and director of the Internet Public Library. Dr. Janes possesses three degrees from Syracuse University, including an M.L.S. and a Ph.D. from the School of Information Studies. He is the co-author of several other books, including *Online Retrieval: A Dialogue of Theory and Practice*, with Geraldene Walker (published by Libraries Unlimited).

Sara Ryan

Sara Ryan is reference services coordinator for the Internet Public Library. She recently received her M.I.L.S. from the University of Michigan. Says Sara, "I used to study medieval manuscripts that were in danger of disintegrating. Now I work in a library that has no building. This is all my parents' fault."

Fred Zimmerman

Frederick Zimmerman lives with wife Cheryl and daughter Kelsey in lovely Ann Arbor, Michigan. He works as a research scientist at the Environmental Research Institute of Michigan (ERIM), where he is assigned to the Consortium for International Earth Science Information Network (CIESIN). In his spare time, he is editor and publisher of the Internet Book Information Center (*http://sunsite.unc.edu/ibic/IBIC homepage.html*).

Stephanie Walker

Stephanie Walker is an information specialist at TradeWave Galaxy in Austin, Texas. She is in charge of redesigning the topic structure of Galaxy as well as adding new entries to the database. Stephanie has a B.A. in English from the University of Southern Mississippi and a Master of Library and Information Science from the University of Texas at Austin. She has a personal web page at: *http://galaxy.einet.net/EINet/steph/index.html*.

Tim Howes

Tim Howes is a senior systems research programmer for the University of Michigan's Information Technology Division. He received a B.S.E. in Aerospace Engineering, an M.S.E. in Computer Engineering, and is currently completing a Ph.D. in Computer Science from U-M. He is project director and principal investigator for the NSF-sponsored WINX project and in charge of directory service development and deployment at U-M. He is the primary architect and implementor of the U-M LDAP and DIXIE directory packages, the GDA X.500 DSA, and a major developer of the QUIPU X.500 implementation. He is author or co-author of many papers and RFCs, including RFC 1777 and RFC 17778 defining the LDAP protocol. He is chair of the IETF Access, Searching, and Indexing of Directories working group, former co-chair of the Integrated Directory Services working group, and an active member of the ACM and IEEE.

Other Titles of Interest in the Neal-Schuman NetGuide Series

THE COMPLETE INTERNET COMPANION FOR LIBRARIANS
By Allen C. Benson

"An effective road map for new drivers on the information superhighway, teaching not only the rules of the road but also showing how to deal with roadblocks and detours." *Library Journal*

1-55570-178-7. 1995. 8 1/2 x 11. 405 pp. $49.95.

LEARNING THE INTERNET:
A Workbook for Beginners
By John Burke

Learn the Internet interactively with this field-tested, hands-on workbook that guides you through all of the Internet basics with creative and detailed activities that will teach you and reinforce your skills—and are fun to do! Using it is like attending a workshop on using the Net, one that will allow you to work at your own pace and at times convenient to you.

1-55570-248-1. 1996. 8 1/2 x 11. 150 pp. $29.95.

THE INTERNET COMPENDIUM: GUIDES TO RESOURCES BY SUBJECT
By Louis Rosenfeld, Joseph Janes, and Martha Vander Kolk

This unique series, compiled by a team from the acclaimed University of Michigan Internet Clearinghouse, provides direct location access to a virtual mall of over 10,000 Internet addresses in hundreds of subjects.

Subject Guides to Humanities Resources
1-55570-218-X. 1995.
8 1/2 x 11. 368 pp. $75.00.

Subject Guides to Health and Science Resources
1-55570-219-8. 1995.
8 1/2 x 11. 529 pp. $75.00.

Subject Guides to Social Sciences, Business, and Law Resources
1-55570-220-1. 1995.
8 1/2 x 11. 424 pp. $75.00.

Buy all three subject guides for $175
1-55570-188-4.

"While indexing the ever-changing environment of the Internet may seem an impossible job, this series makes an excellent start and will be valuable on the reference shelf for both librarians and patrons." *Library Journal*

CONNECTING KIDS AND THE INTERNET: A Handbook for Librarians, Teachers, and Parents
By Allen C. Benson and Linda Fodemski

At last, an Internet guide that teaches school media specialists, teachers, and parents how to naviagate the Net—and provides sample lesson plans that will enable kids to learn, too. It also contains a guide to the best educational and recreational resources for kids.

1-55570-244-9. 1996. 8 1/2 x 11. 300 pp. $35.00.

USING THE WORLD WIDE WEB AND CREATING HOME PAGES:
A How-To-Do-It Manual for Librarians
By Ray E. Metz and Gail Junion-Metz

The first and only manual specifically designed to help you browse the Web, *Using the World Wide Web* demonstrates how to integrate the Web into your library services and build a home page for your library that will be the toast of the electronic community.

1-55570-241-4. 1996. 8 1/2 x 11. 200 pp. $39.95.

REFERENCE & COLLECTION DEVELOPMENT ON THE INTERNET:
A How-To-Do-It Manual for Librarians
By Elizabeth Thomsen

Here is a cutting-edge manual that evaluates and gives librarians the tools to find thousands of different Internet resources that offer guidance in collection development and reference ser-vices. It explains how and where to benefit from online communities, e-mail professional interest groups, Usenet newsgroups, literary groups, FAQs, and electronic texts.

1-55570-243-0. 1996. 8 1/2 x 11. 240 pp. $39.95.

THE INTERNET ACCESS COOKBOOK:
A Librarian's Commonsense Guide to Low-Cost Connections
By Karen G. Schneider

Let *American Libraries'* "Internet Librarian" columnist help you find cost-effective, entry-level solutions for dial-accessible Internet connections! Spiced with tasty charts, tables, graphics, and checklists, the book's "recipes" provide advice for both PC and Mac users.

1-55570-235-X. 1996. 8 1/2 x 11. 332 pp. $24.95

Publication dates, prices, and number of pages for new titles may be estimates and are subject to change.

To order or request further information, contact:

Neal-Schuman Publishers
100 Varick Street, New York, NY 10013
212-925-8650
or fax toll free—1-800-584-2414